THE BREEZY PENTLANDS

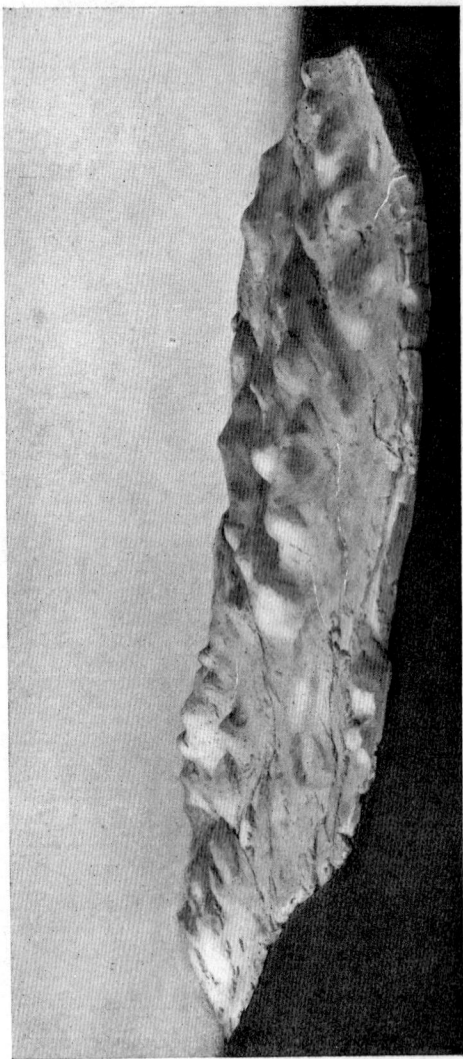

BIRD'S-EYE VIEW OF PENTLAND HILLS

(Looking east from an imaginary point above Cobbinshaw)

Photograph by Drummond Young & Watson, Edinburgh, from a model in the Author's possession

[Frontispiece

THE BREEZY PENTLANDS

BY GEORGE M. REITH, M.A.

T N Foulis
publisher

EDINBURGH AND LONDON . MCMX

3

914.1
3699F

TO MY WIFE

CONTENTS

ILLUSTRATIONS

PREFACE

It is impossible for me to recall, or to make proper acknowledgment to, the many who, by word of mouth and by letter, have contributed to the matter of this volume. To hundreds in the Pentland area I am indebted for much that appears in these pages. I desire, however, to record, with all gratitude, the help given me by Mr William Young, Edinburgh, Mr Ewen Cameron of Rutherford, and Rev. William Smith of Dunsyre, in the compilation of the text.

As for the pictures which illustrate the text, I am under obligations to Mr Hunter Crawford, Mr Edward Drummond Young, both of Edinburgh, and to Mr E. J. Bedford of Eastbourne. Also to Mr James Kinnear, a painter who has done more for the Pentlands than any other artist, and to Sir Edward Moss, for his kind permission to reproduce Crawford's picture, *At the Foot of the Pentlands*.

*
* *

I have not thought it necessary to publish a new map of the Pentland Hills. There is a good map in *The*

Pentland Hills : Their Paths and Passes (W. A. S.), issued by the Scottish Rights of Way Society, Ltd. There is a better map—*The Pedestrians' Pocket Map of the Pentland Hills* (Bartholomew)—better, because it is on a larger scale. This should be used as a companion to the present work. See *Appendix* C (p. 168).

*_**

I have to apologise for the exceeding badness of some hasty water-colour sketches of mine, reproduced in the following pages. They are published (rather against my inclination) on the advice of friends interested in the Pentlands, who think that, in spite of their crudity and roughness, they will prove useful to wanderers on the hills. That is reason enough for me.

*_**

May I add that I shall be grateful to any who will send suggestions, criticisms, corrections, or information of any kind bearing on the Pentland Hills, to 31 Chalmers Street, Edinburgh.

GEORGE M. REITH.

April 1910.

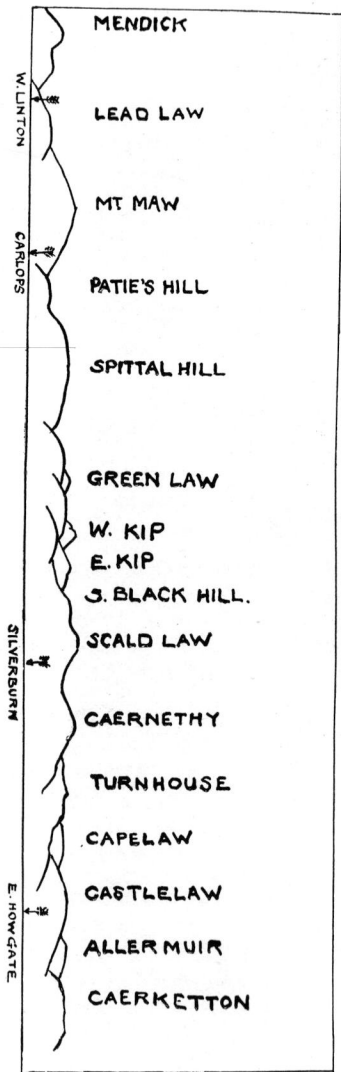

A.

MENDICK

W. LINTON

LEAD LAW

MT MAW

CARLOPS

PATIE'S HILL

SPITTAL HILL

GREEN LAW

W. KIP

E. KIP

S. BLACK HILL.

SILVERBURN

SCALD LAW

CAERNETHY

TURNHOUSE

CAPELAW

E. HOWGATE

CASTLELAW

ALLERMUIR

CAERKETTON

B.

(SWANSTON)

CAERKETTON

ALLERMUIR

CAPELAW

TURNHOUSE

CAERNETHY

SCALD LAW

S. BLACK HILL

E. KIP

W. KIP

GREEN LAW

SPITTAL HILL

COCK RIG

(DORESTANE) (CAULDSTANE SLAP)

WETHER LAW

E. CAIRN HILL

W CAIRN HILL

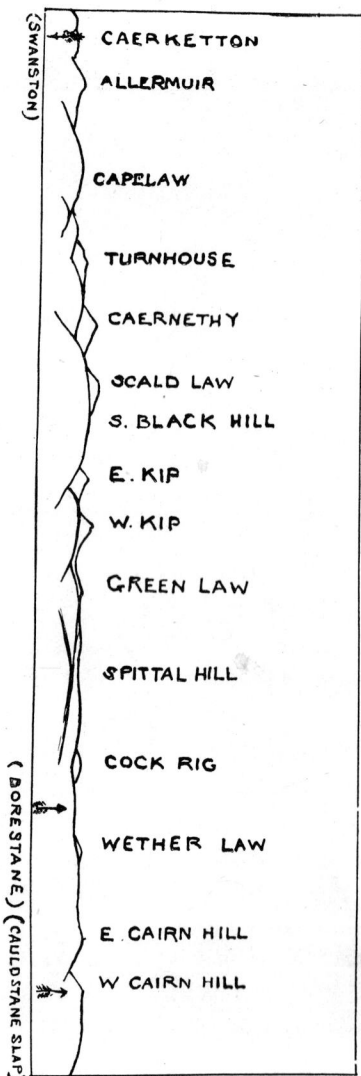

The Pentland Hills as seen from

A.—Cray Brae (Leadburn)
B.—Turnhouse Golf Course

[*To face page* 1

THE
BREEZY   PENTLANDS

CHAPTER I

WHY THIS BOOK IS WRITTEN

EDINBURGH is proud to think herself the finest capital
in Europe, and is mightily pleased with every en-
thusiastic tourist who confirms her opinion. " Beautiful for situation," like the ancient and venerable
fortress-sanctuary among the Judean hills, she possesses many natural advantages denied to cities of
greater size and greater importance in the world's
eye. Her citizens have a wide choice in the matter of
breathing-spaces and playgrounds, many of these
owing little or nothing of their amenities to the hand
of man. One of the greatest of her charms, however,
her citizens know least, and that is the range of hills
which, beginning about three miles from the centre
of the town, and stretching in a south-westerly direction athwart Midlothian, across the northern corner
of Peeblesshire, comes to an end in north-east Lanarkshire. The range, roughly speaking, fills a rectangle of
sixteen miles by four and a half; the highest point,
Scald Law, is 1898 feet above sea-level, while there

A

are at least sixteen other summits whose altitude is over a thousand feet, and three that are only slightly lower than the highest. The Pentlands would be called a mountain-range in England; but as we can see from their peaks and from their northern slopes, in the blue distance across the wide plain watered by the Forth, some of the gigantic bens of the Highlands, whose height can show a yard for the Pentland foot, we are content to speak of them as hills. Yet there are spots amongst those hills where one could easily imagine himself in the heart of the Highlands.

Edinburgh is wonderfully indifferent to the price-less boon she possesses in having the Pentlands so near and so accessible. Comparatively few of her citizens have ever set foot on these heathery slopes. Very few, indeed, born and bred in the capital, could name the peaks they have seen from infancy. This remark has been frequently made before—it is a common-place amongst the select brotherhood of Pentland en-thusiasts—and I repeat it with the emphasis of astonishment. Ignorance alone can account for this apathy. Ignorance!—I once heard a distinguished Edinburgh lawyer, who has the privilege of writing to His Majesty's Signet, inform a party of inquiring strangers that the Pentlands were the Braids! This ignorance and its consequent apathy may be due to the slackness fostered by the conditions of modern city-life, which, by means of railways, tramways, and motors, encourage laziness to such an extent that even districts of the town where these facilities have not penetrated are gradually being considered ungetat-able. The average citizen grumbles if his business takes him to a quarter that gives him the alternatives of walking or taking a cab. To him the Cauldstane Slap seems further off than London—is indeed further off, because it requires greater exertion on his part to get there. So he lives and dies without knowing of the rare pleasaunce Providence has laid out for him within a few miles of his own door. I have fallen into the habit of asking wanderers on these hills whether or no they are Edinburgh-born and Edinburgh-bred. About one in ten says that he is. Yet the Pentlands afford material for the gratification of the natural or acquired tastes of a many-sided life. The zoologist and the botanist will find much to interest them in the life of the region; the geologist and the mineralogist have good things provided for them; the historian and antiquarian have a wide field of research—for relics of a past human life can be traced to a period anterior to the Roman occupation of Britain; the shooting man and the angler have large scope for their sport—many of the fishing grounds are either open or accessible on easy terms; of late years the golfer has invaded some of the outlying spurs with his quaint pick and shovel; the poet and the romancer have been on the hills, and have left that behind them which intensifies the wanderer's delight in the scenes traversed; easel and camera may be carried to many a lovely spot, and the results richly reward the labour expended; even that wisest of created beings, the weather-prophet, may learn something, for, on these hills, a considerable portion of the weather consumed in Edinburgh is manufactured. And there is health in every breath drawn on their breezy heights. I may add that the Scottish Rights-of-Way and Recreation Society, Ltd., has done splendid service as the jealous guardian of public privileges. It has marked the open paths on the range with finger-posts and guiding-poles, and issued a convenient little handbook,* which not only gives details as to routes, but also stimulates the interest of the traveller in the scenes through which he passes.

I may be permitted to express surprise that, apart from this handbook, and a geological work by the late Mr Charles Maclaren,† there is no book on the Pentland Hills, so far as I can ascertain, giving the descriptive information that people desire to guide their thoughts as well as their feet.‡ After a fruitless search for books of the kind, I came to practical agreement with the philosopher who said that, if you cannot find a book on a subject that interests

* *The Pentland Hills : their Paths and Passes*, by W. A. S. (With a Map.) Edinburgh : Macniven & Wallace.

† *Geology of Fife and the Lothians*, by Charles Maclaren, F.R.S.E., F.G.S., &c. Edinburgh : A. & C. Black, 1838. Second edition, 1866. Now out of print.

‡ While the books mentioned above are the only works dealing with the Pentlands directly, it should be mentioned that Brown of Newhall's notes to his edition of Dr Pennicuik's *History of Tweeddale* contain a great deal of matter concerning them ; and also that an illustrated and annotated edition of Allan Ramsay's *Gentle Shepherd*, published in two volumes in 1808, devotes many pages to a detailed description of the range, with special reference to the scenery of the pastoral. Both works are inaccurate in many particulars—especially as to the relative heights of the hills—but they preserve a number of facts, traditions, and notions, which are of great interest to the Pentland enthusiast.

you, you should sit down and write one yourself.* Hence this volume.

Its purpose is to create and foster interest in Edinburgh's great natural playground, by putting together, more or less discursively, notes and impressions, descriptive, historical, physiographical, anecdotical, collected in many a delightful ramble over the Pentlands during the last ten years. It is therefore to be regarded neither as a guidebook to the hills, nor as an exhaustive treatise thereon, but simply as talk about them, reduced to something like order and system by following the main routes around and across the range. I have to crave the reader's indulgence for the personal note in these pages. In their original form, most of the chapters that follow were actually letters, travel-letters written for the *Singapore Free Press*, to give Brither Scots in the Far East an occasional whiff of the auld countree. The manager and the editor of that newspaper have kindly granted me permission to recast the letters, and issue them to the public in this shape. My acknowledgments are due to their courtesy, and hereby paid with all cordiality. But in

* Even the *Encyclopædia Britannica* does not know these hills—at least not as a range deserving an article to itself. That monumental work, however, is weak geographically. It makes amazing blunders in this respect. I may mention one of the most unpardonable of these. The Strait of Sunda is noted as lying between the islands of Bali and Lombok in the Malay Archipelago. Now, since the principal route to China, before the opening of the Suez Canal, was by the Strait of Sunda, *between Sumatra and Java*, there is no excuse for a blunder of the kind. Yet even higher authorities make ludicrous mistakes. I have seen naval charts in which the Straits of Malacca are confounded with the Strait of Macassar. The two straits are about a thousand miles apart.

the recasting of the letters, I deemed it wise to retain the personal element, in the hope that the reader will feel, when he puts this book to the use which the writer intends, that he has a sympathetic companion, whose talk enables him to see and enjoy better the things that Nature among the breezy Pentlands has prepared for those that love her. Permit me, then, to ramble in talk, as I have often rambled a-foot, armed sometimes with golf-clubs, sometimes with a fishing-rod, and sometimes with only a walking-stick, about these miniature Highlands. To me they have acquired what George Eliot calls " that sweet monotony when everything is known, and loved because it is known."

In these days when walking on the roads has become both a dangerous and an exceedingly uncomfortable pastime, owing to the increase of motor traffic, the attention of walkers may well be drawn to regions where they are free from the dust, stench, noise of the motors, and the dangerous carelessness of many of their drivers.

I have not attempted to describe the mansion-houses and castles within the Pentland area, nor to deal with the history of the families that have successively occupied them. That is a very large subject and would require a volume to itself.

Note.—The manuscript of this book was complete when Mr Robert Cochrane's *Pentland Walks* appeared in 1908. It is a work which all lovers of the Pentlands welcome and find useful. The present volume, as readers of both will recognise, is not a rival but a companion to Mr Cochrane's; and while I have had to question, in an occasional note, some of Mr Cochrane's statements, and while he, in future editions, may have to do the same by some of mine, yet our contributions to the scanty literature of the Pentlands are complementary; we have written on the same subject, but have taken different routes through it. I send this volume forth on its mission, under the conviction that there is a rapidly-growing interest in these long-neglected hills.

PART I

ROUND THE HILLS

CHAPTER II

VISITORS to Rome are advised by the useful Baedeker to spend the first day in taking what he calls " an orientation drive " round the city, in order that they may learn their " airts," and get a general idea of the lie of the land. Similarly, I would suggest an orientation tour round the Pentland Hills on the high roads, starting from Edinburgh and going along the south side of the hills *viâ* Hillend, Easter Howgate, Carlops, West Linton and Dunsyre to Carnwath, and returning to Edinburgh, along the north side, by the Lang Whang and Balerno. Choose your vehicle—horse, carriage, cycle or motor; but if you wish to savour the delights of the tour to the full, you will do it on foot. It can be done easily in a day, on horse or wheel, for the distance is under fifty miles; but if you walk, don't be in a hurry; take a week to it, and you will enjoy it the more. A leisurely—I might almost say a lazy—walking-tour has no equal among the pleasures of life.

Sunt quos curriculo pulverem . . . collegisse juvat.

Let some delight to raise the dust in a whirling motor-

8

Drummond Young & Watson]

[Edinburgh

EVENING—END OF THE PENTLANDS

(From an Oil-Painting by E. Drummond Young)

[To face page 8

car; to those who know the healthy and quiet joys of walking, they are as men who would swallow a magnum of champagne at a gulp. There be times when the busy city man envies the tramp, who is, from many points of view, an enviable person. He is not overburdened with work, but that troubles him little. Rent-day has no terrors for him; rates and taxes to him are as though they were not. His wardrobe gives him small concern; by hook or by crook he clothes his unsoaped body in a miscellaneous assortment of articles, not one of which would fetch sixpence at a jumble sale. He solves the bread-problem of the world, so far as he is personally concerned, by throwing himself upon the generosity of his fellowmen. To which he rarely appeals in vain. He gets bread enough and to spare; for we have often seen him stealthily flinging of his superfluity over a hedge or into a ditch. He contrives to indulge in family joys, for have we not frequently observed him exercising his marital privileges in correcting his wife with fist or boot on the public road? His greatest grievance against the existing cosmos is that the wayside inns will not open their bars to him before eight o'clock in the morning. The greatest hardship you can inflict upon him is to compel him to sleep under a roof; possibly because the only kind of roof he knows is that of a police-cell. Otherwise, what a glorious life is his! Always in the open air, indifferent to all meteorological vicissitudes. No duties, no responsibilities, no anxieties, " a heart at leisure from itself "—imagination absolutely refuses to picture an introspective tramp—and all braid Scotland to loaf in! Perhaps the tramp does not view his happy lot from the standpoint of the harassed and worried city man who envies him. Perhaps our keen enjoyment of a few days' loafing in the year is due to the pressure of the laborious days into which they are sandwiched.

> " *Qui fit, Mæcenas, ut nemo, quam sibi sortem,*
> *Seu ratio dederit, seu fors objecerit, illa*
> *Contentus vivat, laudet diversa sequentes ?* " *

Mæcenas, being long dead, offers no answer to this eternal question; so let us proceed.

It is permissible, even to the most ardent pedestrian, to take a car to the Braid Hills, the sooner to escape the *Sturm und Drang* of the Edinburgh streets. It is permissible also, while passing through the Boroughmuir district, once " a field spacious and delightful by the shade of many stately and aged oaks," and that of Morningside, to drop a tear of sensibility over the vanished demesne and the picturesque little village of forty years ago, now buried under piles of ugly tenements and staring shops, and in another generation to be forgotten as completely as the Lang Dykes, or the Lang Gaitt, where Edinburgh of the eighteenth century used to take a stroll o' nights, and breathe the salt-laden breezes from the Forth. Edinburgh still crowds the Lang Gaitt, morning, noon and night, and is justly proud of its amenities, but calls it by the unromantic name of Princes Street.

* Horace : *Serm*. I. 1. The words may be roughly paraphrased by the old Highland proverb : " The wild duck always wants to be in the loch where she isn't."

The Pentlands come into view as we approach the tramway terminus, the north-eastern end of the range, at least, of which the most striking feature is the steep purple craigs of Caerketton,* whose face conveys to the frivolous imagination the whimsical impression that it has been recently scrubbed with emery-paper. To the right of this is the graceful, slightly-inclined cone of Allermuir,† and beyond that again the slopes of Capelaw are visible, and the crags of Torduff and Torphin.

Pentland—*Pictland!* How the name carries us in one wild leap of thought over a chasm of fifteen hundred years and more, to a time when the painted folk awaited the onslaught of the Italian invaders in their strongholds amongst these hills! Here Pict faced Roman; here doughty deeds were done that history has forgotten. Mother Earth has long ago forgiven the quarrels of her children, has buried them and their weapons, has done her best to obliterate all trace of their existence, not quite successfully, for now and then, in our wanderings, we stumble upon some scarcely recognisable remains of a camp or fort, or the ploughshare turns up a relic that provokes the antiquarian to speculate, and the poet to moralise.

* "Kirk Yetton (Caer Ketton, wise men say)."—R. L. Stevenson, *Memories and Portraits.* The wise men are right, as usual. Mr Charles Maclaren writes "Kirk Yetton"; a mis-spelling due to the fact that Scotsmen, and especially Highlanders, often introduce a *y* sound after hard *k* or *g*. It will be remembered how Mr Lavender loved to hear "gyarden" from Sheila's lips in Borva, but shivered at the same sound from Mrs Lavender's in London.

† The heights of all the important summits are given in a note on p. 12.

From the Braid Hills Road we see the unsunned
face of what I have ventured to call the North Mass
of the range.*

The lie of the unseen hills may be indicated by a
line drawn from Fairmilehead police station through

* For convenience' sake I have grouped the Pentland Hills into four
distinct masses, and have named them as under :—

I. *North Mass*, divided from the next group by Dens Cleugh and the
Glencorse Valley, and lying entirely in the county of Midlothian. It
comprises Allermuir (1617 ft.), Castlelaw (1595 ft.), Caerketton (1500
ft.) ; and the following heights under 1500 ft.—Bell's Hill, Capelaw,
Fala Knowe, Harbour Hill, and Woodhouselee Hill.

II. *North Central Mass*, separated from the next by the Bavelaw burn
and the North Esk valley, and also lying entirely within Midlothian. It
contains the highest peaks of the range—Scald Law (1898 ft.) and
Caernethy (1890 ft.) ; and besides these, West Kip (1805 ft.), East Kip,
(1750 ft.), South Black Hill (1750 ft.), Hare Hill (1740 ft.), Turnhouse
Hill (1636 ft.), North Black Hill (1628 ft.), Spittal Hill, Gap Law,
Green Law and Patie's Hill, all slightly over 1500 ft.

III. *South Central Mass*, lying partly in Midlothian and partly in
Peeblesshire. The line of division between this may be taken as the
course of the Baad Park Burn and the Lyne Valley. This group includes
—East Cairn Hill (1839 ft.), The Mount (1762 ft.), Mount Maw (1753
ft.), Wether Law (1695 ft.), and Cock Rig (1517 ft.).

IV. *South Mass*, in which three counties meet—Midlothian, Peeblesshire and Lanarkshire (see p. 150). It contains West Cairn Hill (1844
ft.), Byrehope Mount (1751 ft.), Craigengar (1700 ft.), Fadden Hill (1526
ft.) ; and the following smaller heights between 1500 and 1300 ft.—Black
Hill, Black Law, Darlees Rig, Dunsyre Hill, Harrowes Law, Henshaw
Hill, Kingseat, Mendick, Mid Hill, The Pike, and Weather Law.

This fourth mass might be divided into two, the dividing line being that
of the water-courses of the two Medwyns. The above arrangement is
wholly arbitrary, and is made solely for convenience of reference. Mr
Charles Maclaren, in his *Geology of Fife and the Lothians*, gives the following general description of the range :—"The eastern part of the hills
forms a single massive group for two miles ; beyond this, for the space
of six miles, they divide, and form two parallel chains, whose summits
are about a mile asunder. The western part consists of a large uneven
circular plateau, about five or six miles in diameter, with a southern inclination, and from 1200 to 1400 [feet] in height."

the summit of Allermuir. There is a marvellously extensive view, worth studying on a clear day, to be had from the road behind the police station as you go towards the Hunter's Tryst. One is afraid to say how many counties can be seen in a sweep of the eye. The Forth Valley, Fife and the Lomonds, the Ochils, Ben Ledi, and Ben Voirlich; also mountains so far away as Ben Lomond in Dumbartonshire and Ben More in western Perthshire, the latter only visible, however, when covered with snow.* The extensiveness of the view is remarkable, considering that the altitude of the road at this point is not much over 500 feet above sea-level. In a field close by stands the Kel Stane or Camus Stane, traditionally reported to mark the site of a battle between Picts and Romans, in which the native king was slain. The name *Kel* is ancient British, and means " battle "; *Camus*, on the other hand, is Scandinavian. Two large cairns once stood in the neighbourhood, which, on being removed to make way for the road, were found to contain a large quantity of human bones. Two cairns of a similar description are still standing in the Garvald valley.†

Crossing the Swanston burn by the modern substitute for the auld Bow brig, we are on the skirts of the Pentlands. Half a mile further on, near the little hamlet of Lothianburn, and on the north side of the

---

* This is my impression. I have never been able to descry Ben More from this point except when it was white with snow, on a sunny day, with a north-west wind blowing.

† See p. 155.

Golf Club-house, a by-road leading thither tempts us to turn aside and make for the tiny village of Swanston, which has a reputation out of all proportion to its size, thanks to the magic pen of Robert Louis Stevenson. Village is too big a word to describe it.

Stevenson calls it " a hamlet of some twenty cottages, in the woody fold of a green hill." It is snugly ensconced in a sheltered nook under the Craigs of Caerketton. There are eight slated houses, built on three sides of a quadrangle, on each of which, for luck, is fixed a horse-shoe. (The reason why a horse-shoe is regarded as a bringer of luck or a bulwark against ill has never yet been satisfactorily explained. The most probable explanation is that which sees in the shape of the shoe a distant resemblance to the horns of the moon, and which therefore connects this ancient superstitious practice with the Baal and Astarte worship that once prevailed in these islands.*) Beyond this quadrangle some small thatched cottages are grouped in picturesque irregularity near a little burn; and hard by, in a bower of trees, is the house which Stevenson has made famous, and to which his devotees come—chiefly in the bright summertime—to worship. Above are the spurs and the watercourses on the hills where the shy lad saw his early pictures, and dreamed his youthful dreams.

Returning to the high-road from Swanston, and

* Some would connect the superstition with St Dunstan, who was a blacksmith, and on a legendary occasion " seized the Devil by the nose." The display of a horse-shoe on a door was intended to advise His Satanic Majesty that the house was under the protection of the Saint, and that, if he did not wish another nose-pulling, he had better keep clear.

holding southward, we soon reach a point from which three roads diverge. That to the left leads by the village of Old Pentland to the village of New Pentland; the former is worth a visit. The middle road goes to Penicuik by Glencorse. To the right is our present route, by Hillend. It is for some distance a steep ascent round the back of Caerketton, and, as we toil up the hill-road, there opens up on the left a splendid view of the extensive triangular plain watered by the two Esks. It forms a large part of what geologists call the Dalkeith Coal-Field, between which and our present position are great beds of limestone. To many, however, these unsightly blotches on the landscape have precious associations with so much per cent., with which no natural beauties may be permitted to compete.

Now at the top of this incline—we have risen 200 feet in little more than half a mile—stop and look back. There, to the north-east, like a band of pale blue ribbon, is the Firth of Forth, visible from Arthur Seat to North Berwick, with a hazy suggestion of the coast of Fife beyond it. The clear-cut cone of North Berwick Law is a prominent landmark, and close to it appears the heavy shoulder of the Bass Rock, with Traprain Law a little further to the right. On a very clear day St Abb's Head may be descried. The mass of hills filling the horizon on the right is the Lammermuir range, the north-eastern extremity of what geologists call the Scottish Southern Uplands. In the valley below us many interesting spots can be descried, or their position indicated by one who knows the lie of the land. There is Dalkeith, for instance, where the immortal Mansie Wauch hung out his sign. There are many villages in sight, or just out of sight— Gilmerton, Loanhead, Lasswade (which lies too low to be seen from here), Bonnyrigg—alas, bonnie no longer, since inartistic industry has been suffered to erect rows of workmen's houses that touch the lowest depths of ugliness!—Gorebridge clinging to the hill-side across the valley, and Cockpen, whose *ci-devant* laird's luckless wooing has passed into song.

I have begged my reader-companions' permission to be discursive, and take it for granted; so, while again and again our eyes seek the magnificent panorama of the Forth, as seen from this point, let me insert here a short chapter, which has nothing to do with the Pentland Hills, to say something about the firth that I believe has not been said before.

CHAPTER III

THE SCOTTISH BAY OF NAPLES

" FAR awa' fowls have fair feathers " is a proverb which, with gentle sarcasm, reminds people that they may have at their own doors glories and beauties as worthy of their admiration as anything in the fairy regions of Elsewhere. The near is ever the common-place—"'tis distance lends enchantment to the view."

The Bay of Naples is regarded by all who have seen it as one of the finest combinations of land- and sea-scape in the world. It is conventionally accepted as such by those who have not seen it, and it has become the standard of perfection according to which all similar combinations are judged. One or two places beyond Europe challenge its supremacy in this re-spect. A Sydney man would be slow to admit that his harbour was inferior to anything upon earth. Chilians hold Valparaiso Bay to be without a rival in creation. An American lady, with whom I was once standing at the top of the beautiful pass between Nagasaki and Moji in Japan, publicly recanted her faith in the superiority of the Bay of Naples, as she looked at the sapphire waters of the land-locked harbour far below us, smiling in the rays of the westering sun. And I have had my doubts about the pre-eminence of the Italian bay when looking at the exquisite beauty of the bay at Honolulu, with the rich peacock-blue of its waters acting as a foil to the softer colours of the land, and throwing into relief the pink-and-gold splendours of Diamond Head beyond Wai-ki-ki. But then one has to remember that the perception and enjoyment of natural beauty, and the comparison of a scene present with the memories of scenes elsewhere, depend on the mood of the observer at the time, and that again depends upon many things. There is in Scotland a bay which, to my mind, reproduces some of the main features of the Bay of Naples, although it is not regarded by those who live on its shores as anything out of the common. Familiarity has bred contempt; and as the Brown brothers wonder what Jones sees in their sister Mary, a very ordinary specimen of humanity, that he should be so desperately in love with her, so some worthy fishermen on the coast have expressed their surprise that anyone should be impressed by what wears to them the aspect of monotonous dulness. Yet I never see the bay without feeling that it is one of no ordinary beauty. It seldom wears the deep warm blue of sea and sky which is usually called Italian. Perhaps in the three hot days preceding the thunderstorm, which are said to constitute the average Scottish summer, one may be lucky enough to see it under properly blue conditions—quite different from the hard, cold, steely blue it wears on a bright day in winter or early spring —but, as a rule, its tints are subdued, with a general

tendency towards greyness overhead and a dirty
green beneath.

The bay I refer to is that deep indentation in the
southern shore of the Firth of Forth, which extends,
roughly speaking, from the Pier of Leith to North
Berwick. The coast-line is studded with numerous
towns and villages, with a general resemblance, in
the matter of situation at least, to the chain of little
towns that embroiders the Bay of Naples. My imagination delights to reconstruct the Scottish bay
from the Italian one. The coincidences are rather
striking. Take Arthur Seat as the starting-point. That
prominent landmark is the plug of a pre-historic
volcano, and the geological imagination has little
difficulty in multiplying its height by ten, and filling
the sky-line with a mountain-mass even more impressive and awe-inspiring than Vesuvius. North-
western Edinburgh then becomes Pompeii; Leith,
Torre dell' Annunziata; Portobello, Torre del Greco;
Musselburgh, Resina, the ancient Herculaneum;
Prestonpans, Portici; while the long whinny stretch
of links from Port Seton to Aberlady represents the
site of Naples. North Berwick stands for Pozzuoli;
and the famous Law there has its counterpart in the
Solfatara. Out in the bay, Inchkeith may be roughly
compared to Capri, while Craigleith and Fidra, off
North Berwick, may represent, on a considerably reduced scale, the islands of Procida and Ischia. Curi-
ously enough the bay has no name. At least I have
never heard it called anything but " the Firth," a
name which is applicable to the whole sixty miles of

estuary. It is anonymous also on the map. Sir Walter Scott, however, dubs it Preston Bay in *Marmion*.*

Let no athletic mind leap rashly to the conclusion that I regard this bay as in any sense a serious rival to the Bay of Naples, though I have ventured to connect the two in thought, and point out some remarkable geographical coincidences. Yet the familiar Scottish bay has beauties of its own, visible from many points of view, near and far.

The neighbourhood of the bay has been famous in history from very early times. Legends of Mary, Queen of Scots, abound. Is not Seton Castle there, a favourite resort of hers, where she had staunch friends? In Tranent there is, or was until recently, an ancient roadside ale-house, where the royal lady invariably stopped for a drink when she passed that way. " Bonnie Prince Charlie " has also left his name and his fame in the district, for near the shore of this bay was fought the battle of Prestonpans, where Johnny Cope, coming to teach, was himself taught, " the art of war." The house where the luckless Hanoverian general slept on the night before the battle still stands at Port Seton.

The district, however, has older memories than these. It is celebrated in ecclesiastical legends that go

---

* " Yonder the shores of Fife you saw ;
    Here Preston Bay and Berwick Law,
        And broad between them roll'd,
    The gallant Frith the eye might note
    Whose islands on its bosom float
        Like emeralds chased in gold."

But I never heard this name used locally.

back to the seventh century, if not further. One Baldred,* a zealous missionary in that remote period, was
so beloved by the people of the three parishes of
Aldham, Tyningham and Preston, that when he died,
all three parishes contended for the honour of having
his body to bury. The bishop of the diocese postponed
the funeral, and sent the people to their homes,
counselling them to spend the night in prayer. Next
day, the contending parishioners met at a place pre-
viously agreed upon, and lo, there were three coffins
and three corpses, all exactly alike, so that each
parish got a funeral all to itself, and ever afterwards
maintained, *more humano*, that its corpse was the
only genuine one! Archbishop Spottiswoode's naïve
comment on this legend is worth quoting; he evidently
more than half believes the story—" What policy the
bishop used in this is not known, but hereby we may
see how easily people were in those times led by their
teachers." (Possibly there is here a reflection of the
indocility of the people in the archbishop's own time
to their prelatic teachers.) They learned queer things
in the old days, and were easily satisfied; but one
would like to know where the right reverend gentleman got the other two corpses. The legend reminds
me of a similar one connected with the burial of St
Patrick. I am not quite sure of the details now, but
I read the story long ago in the book of a true be-
liever. Two parties claimed the holy remains, and on
the day of the funeral, the wrong party was misled
by a phantom procession, got up by the angels with

* This was St Baldred, who lived in a hermitage on the Bass Rock.

intent to deceive, while the right party quietly laid
the saint's body in the proper place. It is refreshing
to learn that the angels are not above playing practical jokes on poor humanity, though they are commonly
supposed to frown upon " small deceit and other sin-
ful games." Whatever may have been the offence of
the wrong party, they were at least piously anxious
to do honour to the departed saint, and deserved a
little consideration. But angels (as ecclesiastically
conceived) do not think of trifles of that kind.

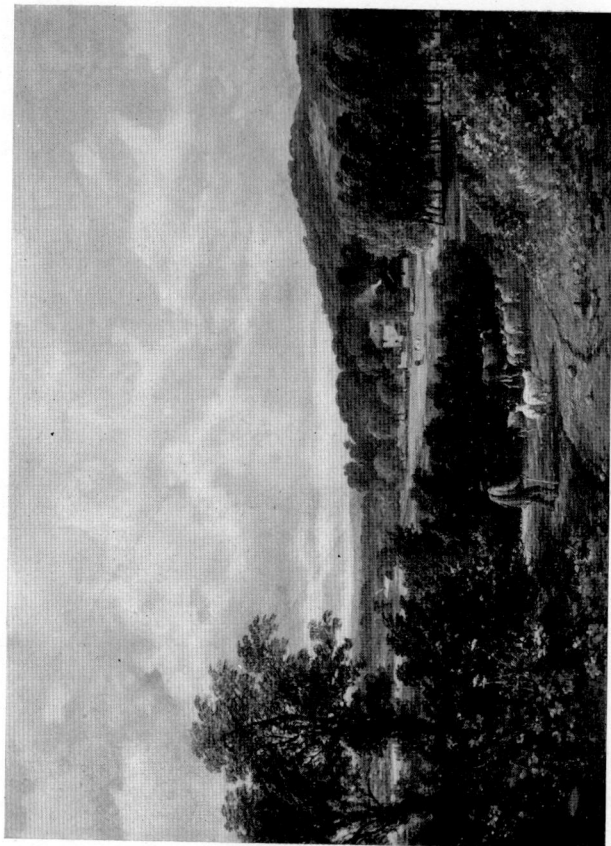

Drummond Young & Watson]   [Edinburgh

AT THE FOOT OF THE PENTLANDS

(From a Painting by the late E. T. Crawford, R.S.A., by kind permission of Sir Edward Moss)

[To face page 22

CHAPTER IV

HILLEND TO RULLION GREEN

PASSING the wooded slopes of Caerketton Hill on the right, we find ourselves skirting the base of Castlelaw, and come to a gateway, opening into an avenue of fine trees, which leads to the mansion house of Woodhouselee. Three and a half centuries ago a house of this name was in the hands of the notorious Hamilton of Bothwellhaugh, who shot the good Regent Moray at Linlithgow in the year 1570. The assassin's crime was the greater by the fact that his victim had spared his life, already forfeit to the law, at the intercession of John Knox. The ruins of the ancient Woodhouselee are to be seen on a crag on the banks of the North Esk River, a little below Auchendinny, over a mile to the southward of our present route. The present house was formerly called Fulford. Old Woodhouselee is interesting on account of one of those romantic lies that have become current in history through the carelessness, or over-carefulness, of annalists. The story goes that the place came to Hamilton through his wife; that after the battle of Langside, in which Hamilton was engaged with the Queen's troops, not only was Bothwellhaugh, his paternal estate, forfeited—there is some doubt on this point too—but his wife's property was also escheated, and handed over to a favourite of the Regent's, who came to Woodhouselee, drove Mrs Hamilton, who had just been confined, from house and home on a cold, winter night, and left her with her child to die of exposure on the bleak hillside. The motive of the story is obvious—to give a colourable pretext, a justifiable reason for Hamilton's abominable crime. But the story is a pure myth. Hamilton's wife was still alive, and residing quietly at Bothwellhaugh, while her husband was in hiding after the murder.* But the *démenti* of the historian has little effect on these romantic traditions, which, like the sylph in the *Rape of the Lock*, when sundered by a snip of the historical shears, heal " at the first intention," and flutter about as gaily as ever.

Beyond Woodhouselee we pass through the little village of Howgate, called Easter Howgate to distinguish it from another village of the same name on the other side of Penicuik. If this be the original of Glenburnie, one is glad to note that, so far as may be judged from outward appearance, the influence of Mrs Mason has survived that of Mrs MacClarty.†

* *See* John Hill Burton, *History of Scotland*, vol. v. p. 14, *note.*—Mr Robert Cochrane repeats this "commonly accepted tradition" in his *Pentland Walks*. It should need no further refutation in a modern critical age.

† *The Cottagers of Glenburnie*, by Elizabeth Hamilton, is now, I fear, a forgotten book in the land of its birth. It belongs to the highly moral class of works represented in England by *Sandford and Merton* and the *Successful Merchant*. Yet there are lively pictures of Scottish rural life

"GLENBURNIE" (EASTER HOWGATE)

[To face page 24

We then descend into the pretty wooded valley between Castlelaw and Turnhouse Hill, past the entrance to the mansion called The Bush, and through the farm-town of Crosshouse,* and get over the Glencorse burn by the ancient, and once picturesque, Flotterstane Brig. The picturesqueness of this old bridge has been wantonly destroyed of recent years by the District Water Trust of Edinburgh. One of the parapets has been removed, and a stiff, ungainly modern structure substituted for it, to carry water-pipes across the valley. One sees no earthly reason why the aqueduct should not have been built a few yards down the stream, and the old bridge left intact; and wonders why no voice was raised in protest against this vandalism while it was a-doing.

It is a puzzle to me why the old Scottish engineers, in carrying a road over a bridge, almost invariably led the road to the bridge in a sharp curve on both sides—a curve that must have been extremely dangerous in the old coaching days, and, in these days of cycles and motors, necessitates the erection of a warning notice. Why did they arrange that the road should cross the bridged valley in this serpentine fashion? One recognises the necessity of a winding road down the slope on both sides, but why were the turns made so sharp just at the bridge? Flotterstane Brig is a case in point, and so are many others that we have to pass in the course of our present journey.

and character that one would not willingly let die. Mrs Mason's moralities are unexceptionable but occasionally irritating. Mrs MacClarty is altogether delightful—as a study.

* See pp. 106, 107.

The road to the right at the north end of the bridge leads up the Glencorse and Loganlee valleys, past the reservoirs bearing these names.*

From Flotterstane Brig we have a stiff pull up, the road rising 300 feet in little more than a mile. If you are on a bicycle, and not in your first youth, you must dismount and foot it. But the stiffness of the pull is more than compensated for by the scenic and historic interest of the district. On the right, a few hundred yards above the bridge, is a quaint old farm called the House of Muir, once the scene of a great cattle and sheep market; and to the left, on the road branching off to Penicuik by Mauricewood, stands a curious old house which goes by the name of Martyrs' Cross. I believe it was some kind of conventual establishment originally, though it is now a private house. Its present name is doubtless derived from the stone cross that surmounts its façade, and from its nearness to the martyrs' tomb. It has no connection, however, with these martyrs. The tomb referred to stands on the green slope of Turnhouse Hill, about half a mile from this point. Here, it may be remembered, Dominie Sampson, whose eccentricities rendered his safe conveyance to Edinburgh by Colonel Mannering and his valet Barnes a matter of no little anxiety, contrived to escape from the carriage, and made for the monument " which was dear to his Presbyterian predilections."† We are in the immediate neighbourhood of

* See pp. 103, 105, 119, etc.

† Scott had " Presbyterian predilections " himself when he was young, but he did his best later to rub this disgraceful blot out of his life and character.

Rullion Green, the scene of one of the desperate battles
of the Covenanting period.

Permit me to exercise here the privileges of the
discursive, and gossip a little about this battle. It was
one of the events of John Dryden's *Annus Mirabilis*,
though I scarcely think he would have included it
amongst the *mirabilia* of the year (1666). At anyrate
he did not. It was in the days of the " Merrie Monarch," whose reign was so calamitous to his hapless
subjects in the north. It was the end of a little splutter
of rebellion, generally known in history as the Pentland Rising. The name is misleading, for though the
rebellion was actually crushed at this spot, it broke
out in Galloway, where Sir James Turner and his
gentle dragoons were endeavouring, by the Christian
persuasions of sword and pistol, to convert reluctant
Scottish Presbyterians to Episcopacy. The pious
Charles II. had declared that Presbyterianism was no
fit religion for a gentleman, to which dictum all Presbyterians will heartily subscribe, if Old Rowley himself be taken as the moral standard of gentility. The
policy of his government was to compel the Scottish
people to conform to English notions and practices
in religion, whether they liked them or not; and military force was added to the ineffectual spiritual
suasions of the curates to further this laudable design.
But how slow men are to recognise the benevolent
intentions of their superiors! Scotland might by this
time have had a religion fit for gentlemen—of a kind
—had this Charles of blessed memory been permitted
by Providence to have his own way.

Nothing—not even patriotism—can excuse the obstinacy of the Scotch in refusing to fall in with these plans for their moral and spiritual improvement; and nothing can palliate, in the eyes of the enlightened and cultured historian of to-day, the resistance they offered to their king's clerical and military emissaries, no matter how great the provocation they received. Sir James Turner served his royal master with the most praiseworthy zeal, and of course reaped the reward of his fidelity and enthusiasm in the violent dislike of the people of Galloway. One day some of his dragoons in the village of Dalry had stripped an old man, and were playfully proceeding to roast him on a red-hot gridiron, for the brutal crime of refusing to attend the ministrations of the episcopal curate in the parish church, and aggravating that crime by declining to pay the fine which the law of the land levied on such recusants. But some peasants over-heard the wicked old man's cries, and could not endure the sight of his well-deserved sufferings. The cowardly ruffians deforced the soldiers in the execution of their lawful duties, and made them prisoners. Elated by their success, the peasants marched to Dumfries, their numbers rapidly increasing as they went, with the object of getting hold of Sir James Turner. So swiftly did they move on his headquarters that they got him in his night-shirt; and in response to his cries for mercy, backed by evidence which he produced to show that the playful brutalities of his soldiers were against his general orders for leniency, they spared his life, but made him a prisoner, and

took him with them on the expedition they now
meditated. From Dumfries the insurgents marched
through Ayrshire to Lanark, and thence towards Edinburgh by Bathgate, across the great moor that skirts
the northern base of the Pentlands. They were an
undisciplined rabble to begin with, about 3000 strong,
under the command of Colonel Wallace, who had only
little time to lick his raw recruits into shape. Yet Sir
James Turner, in his interesting memoirs, has left on
record his surprise at the rapidity with which these
peasants learned military discipline, and his admiration of their leader's skill. It was the month of November, the weather was wild and wet, and the march
across the moor under these conditions extremely trying. Many deserted and made for their homes. The
rebels hoped to excite the sympathy of the citizens of
Edinburgh in their behalf; and undoubtedly they had
much sympathy there, but the civic authorities and
the legal fraternity were strongly against them. When
they reached Colinton they learned that the terrible
General Dalzell of Binns was pressing on their rear
with a strong force, was actually at Currie, only three
miles off, and that Edinburgh, the city of their hopes,
was prepared to resist them. They therefore hastily
withdrew round the north-eastern end of the Pentlands to the eastern ridge of Turnhouse Hill, and a-
waited the appearance of the enemy. Dalzell was a
savage Royalist who had studied the art of war and the
graces of civilisation in Russia. He had refused to al-
low a razor to touch his face since the execution of
Charles I., and the fierce, shaggy-bearded veteran was

an object of superstitious terror to the peasantry of Scotland, who dubbed him the " Muscovie Beast." He certainly gave them no cause to reverence either his person or his memory. The battle was prolonged, but its issue was inevitable. The advantage lay with the insurgents at first, for it is difficult to operate with cavalry on a steep slope against men intrenched above them; but the superior numbers and discipline of Dalzell's troops told in the end. The last assault of the Royalists was made just after sunset. Wallace's force was routed, leaving about fifty dead in the field, and more than twice that number of wounded and prisoners in the hands of the enemy. The prisoners were taken to Edinburgh, and though on the field they were promised their lives if they surrendered, more than thirty of them were put to death, after being subjected to horrible tortures.* Hugh M'Kail, the original of Ephraim MacBriar in *Old Mortality*, was one of these unfortunates. A crowd of women from Edinburgh carried their household linen to the scene of the battle, made shrouds for the dead, and buried the bodies of these ill-fated Covenanters in a grave which is marked by the present monument. From year to year a memorial service for these poor deluded fanatics, who would not accept a religion fit for gentlemen, either at the hands of their gracious monarch or at the pistols of his dragoons, is held at Rullion Green, generally on a Sunday evening in August, and is attended by large

* "Shields, Kirkton, and Wodrow allege that the king wrote to stop the execution, but that Sharp kept up the letter."—*Scottish History and Life*.

crowds from many miles around, whose interest may be neither purely patriotic nor eminently religious. The service in these wild surroundings is highly impressive, however, and deepens interest in this mountain-sanctuary, hallowed by the memory of those men of old (blind fanatics, of course!) who flung away their lives for the liberties of their country and their Church.

CHAPTER V

RULLION GREEN TO CARLOPS

WE return to the high-road, and shortly after passing Marchwell, which looks like a wayside inn but isn't, we reach the summit of the long steep incline. The road at this point attains an altitude of 900 feet, and keeps about that level, with slight variations, for nearly five miles. It is of that easy, undulating character which, combined with a fine surface, the cyclist loves. And here the traveller, whether on foot or on wheel, begins to taste the intoxicating richness of the Pentland air. Flabby lungs, accustomed to inhale the thin and gritty atmosphere of the city, instinctively expand, and drawing in deep, long breaths, begin to tingle with healthy pleasure; one's eyes brighten, and there is a new thrill in every nerve. The scenery, too, becomes wilder and grander. The road hugs the side of the hills, and runs high above the wooded North Esk valley, where over the trees can be seen the tops of the Penicuik factory chimneys vomiting forth long streams of black smoke, beyond which again the Muirfoot* Hills fill in the horizon. To the right rise four great heights of the North Central Mass—Turnhouse,

---

* Dr Chambers in his *History of Peeblesshire* (1864), assigns a Danish origin to this name, and takes it as a corruption of Morthwaite.

32

Drummond Young & Watson]

NEAR SALTERSYKE

[Edinburgh

[To face page 32

Caernethy, Scald Law and the South Black Hill, a fine mountain rampart, intersected by deep ravines. No rock is visible, but a fine mantle of green turf, patched with the purples, browns and greys of heather, clothes the hills to the top. The view backward also is very fine. The mouth of the Firth of Forth is visible—to say nothing of the stretch of field and woodland between—with North Berwick Law, the Bass Rock and Traprain Law standing out boldly against the eastern sky-line.

At the mouth of the ravine between Scald Law and the South Black Hill stands the hamlet of Silverburn, whence there is a picturesque by-road leading to Penicuik, and where there stands a little dairy-farm which the thirsty pedestrian or cyclist may visit with advantage. A merry reminiscence flashes across my mind at this point. A party of cyclists sought refreshment at this " howff " ten years ago, or more, and was received by a buxom dairy-maid with " her golden hair hanging down her back," and an assortment of hairpins in her mouth. She supplied us with foaming beakers of milk, and while we discussed these she calmly proceeded with her toilet before a little scrap of mirror on the wall. A festive member of the party begged for a lock of her hair as a souvenir of the occasion. Nothing embarrassed by the tender request and the trying publicity he had given it, the damsel turned and said: " Ye can hae it a', gin ye like! " The forward youth, not expecting an offer of the whole season's crop, and being somewhat in the position of the " Wee Frees " when they got more than they could comfort-

C

ably manage, explained shamefacedly that he would
in that case take the will for the deed, and resumed
his journey under a heavy fire of chaff from his com-
panions. This reminiscence suggests that Silverburn
might be considered a suitable *locus* for the tragi-
comedy of the following ballad:—

TIBBIE.

O Tibbie is oor dairymaid, a sonsy, gawsy quean,
   There isna wilder hempie in the shire :
She's got the verra—imphm—o' a sparkle in her een ;
    Ay, Tibbie wad the blatest bard inspire.
      O Tibbie wad the blatest bard inspire ;
      O Tibbie wad the blatest bard inspire ;
      Ay, Tibbie wad the blatest bard inspire
        An' that's what's ailin' me !

When Tibbie drives the kye at morn, or nichtly caa's them
    hame,
   Her kilted coaties a' the lads admire ;
An' whan she stauns oot-bye the door her bonnie locks to kaim,
   O Tibbie sets a monie hairts a-fire !
      O Tibbie sets a monie hairts a-fire ;
      O Tibbie sets a monie hairts a-fire ;
      Ay, Tibbie sets a monie hairts a-fire,
        An' that's what's ailin' me !

An' ilka Sawbath-day she drives the birkies fairly daft ;
   The mennister she ogles frae the choir,
Whiles keekin' at the callants in the forebriest o' the laft,—
   The Laird himsel' to Tibbie micht aspire !
      Ay, he himsel' to Tibbie micht aspire ;
      His vera sel' to Tibbie micht aspire ;
      The Laird himsel' to Tibbie micht aspire,
        An' that's what's ailin' me !

For Tibbie, blithesome Tibbie, O ma greinin' hairt was fain ;
   O' dawtin' her methocht I cudna tire ;

But wow, ae waefu' day I gaed to ask her for ma ain,
An' fand her kissin' Postie in the byre !
   O Tibbie kissin' Postie in the byre !
   Ah, Tibbie kissin' Postie in the byre !
   Ay, Tibbie kissin' Postie in the byre !
      An' that's what's ailin' me !

The road now sweeps gently downward round the
base of the South Black Hill, and across the mouth
of the valley formed by that hill with the two Kips
and Gap Law. The roofless farmhouse of Saltersyke,
seen on the right, stands in a track which winds up
the east side of the valley to the pass across the shoulder of the West Kip,* and thence descends to Balerno
via Bavelaw. A small section of the old Biggar road
—a few hundred yards long—is visible from the ruins
of Saltersyke† to Eight-Mile-Burn (or Harkin Burn),
which is now only a geographical name, but preserves
the memory of an obsolete system of measurement,
for the old road here crosses a streamlet eight miles
Scots from Edinburgh—say $10\frac{1}{4}$ English miles. The
view on our starboard quarter (so to speak) at this
point is striking. The two Kips‡ are in full view; their
clear-cut peaks and light colours are thrown into
strong and agreeable contrast by the heavy round
shoulder and sombre hues of the Black Hill, and by
the darksome woods of fir and pine on Gap Law. To
the left, for miles, there stretches away the bleak ex-

* See p. 121.

† This " cottage, from the rill on the edge of which it stands, and the
employment of its first inhabitant in bringing salt from the Frith of Forth,
and selling it about the country, is known by the name of the Salter's
Syke."—Brown's *Notes on Pennicuik*.

‡ " Kip " is Anglo-Saxon for peak.

panse of the Auchencorth Moss, where Pict met Pict, and probably also Roman, in battle array, before the dawn of Scottish history.

At Walstone farm, where the Penicuik road joins the highway, the old Biggar road again becomes traceable, at a distance of 200 feet or so to the right, along the base of the Spittal Hill, passing through the little hamlet of Nine-Mile-Burn, and rejoining the present turnpike near Carlops. Nine-Mile-Burn * consists of a few houses in the neighbourhood of the Monks' burn, which rises in the gully between Gap Law and the Spittal Hill, and the district contains various names which enshrine traditions of pre-Reformation times. This will be dealt with further on. The traditions themselves have disappeared; the names are like fossiliferous rocks containing the relics of a life not only extinct but forgotten.† The hamlet contains an old-fashioned inn, which, when this road was the only highway, evidently was a stopping-place for stage-coaches and other vehicles. When one notes the number of inns on these old Scottish roads—they are often little more than a mile apart—one wonders whether their frequency indicates great sluggishness of pace on the part of the horses, or great recurrency of thirst on the part of the passengers in the good old days. Nine-Mile-Burn is connected with at least one distinguished Scotsman, the brilliant young architect, George Meikle Kemp, whose father was a

* So called because it is nine Scots miles (11¾ English) from Edinburgh.

† See Chap. XIII. p. 114.

shepherd in this neighbourhood, and whose wonderful monument to Sir Walter Scott in Edinburgh keeps his own memory green.* Leaving Nine-Mile-Burn, the main-road passes through a belt of trees, and the entrance to New Hall House, in the grounds of which lies Habbie's Howe,† made eternally famous by Allan Ramsay. The Howe is entered by a cart-road a few hundred yards further on, which leads down to a bonnie glade, where the North Esk, under a canopy of fine old trees, sweeps round the skirts of a charming haugh much used by trippers as a banqueting hall, and thence takes its winding way between steep banks, through a narrow, thickly-wooded dell. This is "Habbie's Howe,"

> "Where a' that's sweet in spring and summer grow ;
> There 'tween twa birks, out-ower a little lin,
> The water fa's, and maks a singin' din ;
> A pool breast-deep beneath, as clear as glass,
> Kisses in easy whirls the bord'ring grass."

A footpath skirts the river-bank, now on one side and now on the other; there are picturesque little rustic bridges across the stream, from whose platforms we can see the most charming combinations of scenery, and a very fairyland of light and colour. Little change has passed over this sweet spot since Ramsay wrote,

* Mr Robert Cochrane repeats the popular mistake about the birthplace of G. M. Kemp. He was not born at Moorfoot but at Hillrigg, near Biggar. His birth took place on the removal term-day, and his parents had to stay on for a short time at Hillrigg ere the mother was able to move with her child to their new quarters at Howburn, in the parish of Walston. The boy attended West Linton school from Walston. The father's last removal was to Freretown o' Spittal at Nine-Mile-Burn.

† *i.e.* "Halbert's Hollow."

and peopled it with the lads and lasses of the Merrie Monarch's time. The proprietor, while admitting the public, under certain reasonable restrictions, takes pains to preserve its amenities. It is much patronised by picnickers in the summer-time, and on their account no modern Peggy or Jenny dare now bathe in that limpid pool " when the day grows het."

Returning to the main-road, we proceed on a downward slope, with Patie's Hill on the right, and on the left, Scroggy Brae, a steep bank on the other side of the river, above which stands the farm of Roger's Rig. We cross the North Esk by a stone bridge, which marks the boundary between the counties of Midlothian and Peebles, and find ourselves entering the quaint and picturesque mountain village of Carlops, where the cheery hostess of the Allan Ramsay Hotel* gives us a kindly welcome to her board, and where we shall pause for a while to look at the neighbourhood that cast its spell on the soul of the Edinburgh wigmaker, and by him has been made notable for all time.

---

* There are two inns with provender and accommodation for man and beast. The " Allan Ramsay" is licensed, the other—M'Gill's—is not. As one who delights to roam about the Pentlands at all seasons, I may be permitted to express both surprise and disappointment that there is no inn —licensed or unlicensed—where pedestrians can have a meal and spend the night on the hill-road between Edinburgh and Carlops. There are many spots about the range where the pedestrian would like to stop and spend a day or two, without trenching on the hospitality of local farmers, but our absurd licensing-laws, devised mainly for the reformation of incurable city wastrels, now render these impossible. There used to be at least half a dozen inns—namely, at Lothianburn, Woodhouselee, Easter Howgate, Marchwell, Nine-Mile-Burn and New House (on the old road below Patie's Hill). There may have been others. Nine-Mile-Burn inn has only a six days' license.

CHAPTER VI

CARLOPS

THE neighbourhood of Carlops has been glorified by
the genius of Allan Ramsay. Everybody has at least
heard of Edinburgh's pet poet of the early eighteenth
century, though comparatively few have read his
works. Fewer still are those who can read these without incessant and irritating recourse to the glossary.
" Honest Allan, at whose lamp Burns lighted his brilliant torch," as Sir Walter says, wrote in the nervous
Scottish dialect of his day and environment. His best-
known work is the romantic pastoral comedy called
The Gentle Shepherd, which, until they have read it,
most people suppose to treat of a lamb-like tender of
sheep. Its hero, however, is a shepherd of gentle birth.
Round a very simple, almost commonplace, plot
Ramsay wove a poetical romance of singular beauty,
intensely human and racy of the soil. One can hardly
believe, in reading the work in its final form, that a
large part of it was published in detached fragments,
on broad sheets, and that the poet had at first no idea
as to whither his fancy was leading him. The scenery
of this mystic drama is Habbie's Howe and the neighbourhood of Carlops generally.* Through his *Gentle*

* See p. 37.

Shepherd Ramsay has become a kind of godfather to the farms and landmarks of the whole district, for there are to be seen here and there over the country-side places bearing names such as these—Patie's Hill and Patie's Mill, Roger's Rig, Jenny's Brae, Peggy's Lea, The Lonely Bield, etc.

I confess to peculiar delight in visiting Carlops, and roaming idly about the hills and glens that surround it, enjoying the glorious air, which is like a merry heart, for it " doeth good like a medicine," enjoying also the restfulness and tranquillity of this old-world spot, that kind of quiet so difficult to find in these days of hurry and rush, and so welcome when found. Often, as the long twilight of the summer evenings was closing in, I have strolled about the village green, watching the successors of Patie, Roger and Bauldy at their favourite sport, under the roguish eyes of the modern Peggy, Jenny and Neps. They call it " kites." The superior Englishman calls it quoits, but the best English *discoboli* would find these villagers tough opponents in a match, for they are no mean players. The village lies in a bowl-shaped depression on the hillside, nearly 1000 feet above sea-level. It is completely shut in by a rampart of low hills, and the diameter of the hollow is so small that a vivid imagination, aided by local stimulants, might easily fancy a witch, with or without a broomstick, taking a flying leap from one hill crest to another, clearing the village below at a single bound. This is, indeed, the commonly-received derivation of the name Carlops, or " The Carlops," as it is locally called—the Carline's (witch's) Loup.

Another theory is that the name is a corruption of *Caer Luib* (the fort on the round hill), and it is supposed that traces of Pictish fortifications on a hill standing to the east of the village street lend colour to this. Who shall decide when philologists disagree? Yet I have the audacity to suggest two other possible derivations. In the year 1334 the hapless Edward Baliol ceded part of Peeblesshire to Edward III. of England. The transaction is thus alluded to in Andrew of Wyntoun's *Orygynale Cronykil* (*cir.* 1400):

> "At Karlynlippis and at Crosscryne
> Thare thai made the marches syne." *

The second half of the name in this couplet suggests " lips," not " leaps."† At the southern end of the village stand two crags of porphyrite that have been quarried for generations. They are now about 200 yards apart, but within the memory of some still living there was only the breadth of the road between their faces, and at local festivals—marriages and the like—a rope hung with decorations was slung between the two crests. Before that again, until the present road was widened, the pathway between the crags was so narrow that two carts could not pass in it. It is not impossible that this narrow slap suggested to the rustic imagination lips slightly parted. To call them the witch's lips would be an easy transition. In favour of this theory, I would point out that it is the only one that explains the final *s* in the name. A different spelling appears in Blaev's *Theatrum Orbis Terrarum*

---

* See *History of Peeblesshire*, by Dr William Chambers.

† In Brown's *Notes on Pennicuik* the name is spelled " Caerlips."

(1654), which contains the work of the indefatigable Scottish geographer of the seventeenth century, Rev. Timothy Pont, sometime minister of Dunnet in Caithness. This man personally surveyed all braid Scotland, and drew a series of maps which, in spite of the imperfect implements of that age, and the limitations of a single observer, are remarkable for their general accuracy. Pont spells the name Karlinghoups, and also, it may be added, places the village in Midlothian.* Now the termination *hope* is Saxon, and designates a narrow valley amongst hills. Possibly then the name was Carlinghope or Carlinhope, though this does not explain the final *s*. The village, however, standing as it does in a centre whence several *hopes* radiate into the neighbouring hills, might have been called the Carlinghopes † on that account. My own preference is for the Carline's Lips.

Two rows of neat, white-washed cottages facing each other, skirting the high road for a quarter of a mile, and widening in the middle into the green or common above-mentioned, and a few farmhouses perched on the hillsides round about, constitute the village of Carlops. By the green stands the old-fashioned Allan Ramsay Hotel, the terminus of the Edinburgh coaches and motor *char-à-bancs* that come daily in summer, and a rest-and-be-thankful for an endless stream of cyclists, motorists and pedestrians. On the stone lintel over the low door is carved the

* Blaev's reproduction of Timothy Pont's map of Peeblesshire may be seen in facsimile in Dr Chambers' work cited above.

† See also p. 105, *note*.

date 1792, while a few feet higher there is an ancient, weather-beaten sign-board, which on closer inspection is seen to carry a faded portrait of the poet who has given his name to the hostelry, executed by some artist unknown to fame. On the wall hard by hangs another board bearing a fancy portrait of Mause (the witch in *The Gentle Shepherd*), with the hardly legible legend:

> "The open field; a cottage in a glen;
> An auld wife spinnin' at the sunny en';
> At a sma' distance, by a blasted tree—
> Mausie—a witch . . ."

This work of art is locally attributed to Allan Ramsay, junior, the son of the poet, but a little judicious scepticism is permissible here.*

The scenery of the district must have changed considerably since the eighteenth century, for the woods celebrated in *The Gentle Shepherd* are now scarcely a memory, and the mountain streams whose

> "spate may bear away
> Frae aff the howms your dainty rucks o' hay"—

well, the streams are there still, but no spate can now render them dangerous to flock or crop, for every drop of their waters is pre-empted and regulated for the use of Penicuik in the valley below.

A few visitors spend the summer months in Carlops, but the accommodation is limited and of the simplest character. It is none the worse for that. If the village were more accessible and in closer touch with the busy

---

* I am informed, however, that artists of high standing in those days did not consider sign-painting beneath them.

world, it would be more patronised by the health-seeking townsman. For the last few years coaches and motors have been running daily from Edinburgh during the summer, and these are rapidly making the place and its amenities known. Meanwhile, its scanty house-accommodation, and its distance from railway and telegraph—over three miles—render it inconvenient to many who would otherwise seek summer quarters there. Some of us, however, for abominably selfish reasons, mildly hope that these inconveniences will not be removed yet a while. A popularity entailing much new building and a crowd of summer residents would destroy the charm of this quaint old place in the eyes of those who love it best as it is.

Carlops enjoys a fairly respectable antiquity. Its site was old ere Scottish history began to be written. The Picts were here, of course; they have left traces of their primitive military works on the hillside. It is not improbable that the Romans were here also. Later, in the turbulent days when men were never happy unless they were fighting, there was a tower in the neighbourhood on which stood a beacon whereby alarms might be signalled to and from lower Tweeddale *via* Halmyre and Romanno, with a pillar of smoke by day, or a pillar of fire by night. There is a tradition that one of those mediæval religious eccentrics, who seek Heaven's favour by refusing to be what their Creator meant them to be, lived for many years as a hermit in a cell somewhere on the hill behind the present Temperance Hotel. (I make no comment on the juxtaposition of the sites.) The existing village was founded in 1784 to work the stone and other minerals of the district. There was also " a large influx of weavers, who were tempted by the excellent situation, by the prospect of a near market, and by the inducement of having each one a piece of land attached to his cottage." No stirring event in history is associated with the name of this village. It lives its quiet life in the solitude of the hills, and something of the restfulness of the place steals over the spirit of the visitor as he idles about the district. Should I ever have a nervous breakdown there is no spot in Scotland whither I should betake myself with more hopefulness to rest and recruit. It is impossible to convey in words the quiet delight which an objectless ramble in these solitudes affords me. I call it objectless, because, though I generally carry a fishing-rod in my hand, it has often as much to do with the ramble as Mr Wemmick's on a certain interesting occasion. Often it lies otiose by my side, while at full length on a grassy slope I let Nature's myriad voices murmur in a passive ear, in a lazy enjoyment untroubled by the cares of thought. Some men would slip a book into their pockets as they went to such lonely haunts, but I am of Elia's opinion, " I am not much a friend to out-of-doors reading. I cannot settle my spirits to it." However, I don't agree with Elia's further remark, " If there be a regal solitude, it is a sick-bed." The invalid would, as a rule, be alone, but cannot. He resents in spirit, though his gratitude for manifestly kind intentions restrains the utterance of his resentment, the persistent and sometimes fussy attentions that his prostrate condition invites from compassion-ate health. The " regal solitude," to my mind, is that which you can enjoy in the infrequent interstices of leisure in a busy life in such tranquil spots as these. In the city, after the exhausting strain of the day's crowded life, your weariness darkens the complexion of your thought, and you murmur to yourself through the dreary, wakeful hours of night, " The world is a mistake, and I am the biggest mistake in it! " But here, face to face with Nature in her gentler moods, within ear-shot of the plashing stream, whose every ripple sings a different note, on the green slope that breathes the fragrance of bog-myrtle and heather, you would not have the world other than it is, and are glad to be alive to it.

CHAPTER VII

CARLOPS (*continued*)

ONE could spend a considerable time in Carlops without exhausting the interest of the many walks and rambles open to the pedestrian within (say) a six-mile radius of the village.

Habbie's Howe has been already described.* The entrance to it is only a few minutes' walk from the village, and the journey to the foot of the Howe and back can be done in an hour. The walk can be extended in two directions. Having reached the Monks' Haugh, which begins beyond the point where the Harlawmuir burn joins the Esk, one can strike up the steep side of the ravine across country to the sombre little loch of Marfield, which has a grim reputation in the district, which, however, seems forgotten when the ice is bearing and the " dirl " of the curling-stones makes music in the wintry air. Robert Sanderson, the West Linton poet, has a pathetic ballad on one of the tragedies that occurred there, entitled " The Blossoms in her Hair."†
From Marfield a cart-road leads to Nine-Mile-Burn,‡

---

* See p. 37, *et seq.*

† See *Frae the Lyne Valley: Poems and Sketches*, by Robert Sanderson, 1888. The late Robert Sanderson was Inspector of Poor in the Parish of Linton, and enjoyed more than a local reputation as a poet. He died in 1903.

‡ See p. 36.

whence one has a choice between the old road and the new to return to Carlops. Another extension of the walk through the Howe is to turn to the right on emerging, and skirt the near bank of the Harlawmuir burn till a small farmhouse, known as " The Lonely Bield," is reached. The name, of course, is borrowed from Allan Ramsay. Here lived for many years one of those gifted, self-taught men that are not uncommon in the ranks of the Scottish peasantry—" Molie " Farquharson. His knowledge of history, tradition, antiquities and geology, like Sam Weller's knowledge of London, was " extensive and peculiar." It was not systematised or scientifically arranged, but it was of the kind that made his conversation a thing eagerly sought for by visitors to the neighbourhood. Near Farquharson's old home the Harlawmuir burn is joined by the Carlops burn, which rises in the southern slope of Mount Maw, and a few hundred yards higher up by the Coal burn. At this latter junction there stands a crag of crumbling millstone grit known as the Harbour Craig, so-called because refugees from Rullion Green found there a temporary hiding-place. It was also known, in older times, as the Lover's Loup, and there is an alleged reference to it in *The Gentle Shepherd*, when Patie says to Roger:

> " Yonder's a craig—sin' ye hae tint a' houp,
>   Gae till't your wa's, and tak the lover's loup."

While some ancient romance probably lies hidden in the latter name, the former preserves traditions of the Covenanting period. A glance at the surrounding country shows how eminently suited this spot was for

the holding of conventicles, when such gatherings
were liable to be surprised by the dragoons. The two
burns that meet here flow at the bottom of deep
sykes or gulches some fifty feet below the general
level of the country; in the angle of their confluence,
at the base of the Harbour Craig, there is an undulating stretch of green sward, capable of accommodating
several thousand worshippers at a conventicle, and
these would be invisible to anyone not actually standing on the ridges above. Dragoons might be scouring
the neighbourhood, and might pass within a few
hundred yards of the spot without being aware of
their presence. A grassy platform in front of the Harbour Craig made an excellent pulpit, commanding the
whole *enclave*. The crag itself is carved with many
names, initials and dates, ancient and modern. The
significant dates of 1662, 1666 and 1669 occur frequently. As at Rullion Green, summer " conventicles "
are occasionaly held here, promoted by those who
desire to keep the memory of the Covenanters green.
Now that the Scots Greys, the modern representatives
of the seventeenth-century dragoons, have been per-
manently withdrawn to England, no danger, except
from sudden changes of weather, attends those who
gather at these. Scrambling to the top of the ridge beyond we see a wide expanse of bleak moorland, intersected by deep sykes, across which, either in a bee-
line, or by one of several tracks, we find our way back
to Carlops.

Two other walks may be mentioned, exclusive of
those over the range, which will be described later. A

D

little to the south of the village a road turns to the left, and holds in a south-easterly direction; and taking this, one has the choice of two not uninteresting routes, which afford a fair idea of the general character of the elevated mossy table-land that separates the Pentlands from the western spurs of the Muirfoots, alluded to in a previous chapter (p. 33). The road is very rough and steep in parts, and hardly suitable for cycling, though I have risked it more than once. But there was frequent need for dismounting and ingloriously pushing the machine. The table-land—Auchencorth Moss and Harlawmuir form part of it—keeps in the main an altitude of between eight and nine hundred feet above sea-level, and the streams that drain it, mostly flowing, as indicated above, through deep ravines, empty themselves either into the North Esk, or into the Tweed *viâ* the Lyne. At Deepsykehead there is a cross-road leading, on the left, to Harlaw Muir, and beyond that to Penicuik, and on the right to West Linton by Whitefield and Deanfoot. From Carlops to West Linton by Deepsykehead and back by either the old or the new road (or *vice versâ*) makes a pleasant circular walk of a few hours.* The other walk is to hold straight on past Deepsykehead to Macbie Hill railway station, thence by Macbie Hill House to the road from Leadburn to Broughton. Passing Noblehouse and Halmyre, one reaches West Linton by a cross-country road, almost parallel to

* If the new road between West Linton and Carlops be taken the distance is about 8 miles.   To take the old road increases the distance to 9 miles.

that by which he has come from Carlops. This walk may be somewhat shortened by taking a track which leaves the road opposite Noblehouse, makes for Halmyre wood, and going through that strikes the road again above Broomlee.* Macbie Hill has been known by several names in the course of history— Coitquoitt, Coldevat, Coalyburn. The name Coalyburn is still retained by the streamlet that flows under the road near the railway station. In a plantation hard by may be seen the smallest coal-pit in Scotland (it can be worked by one man), which has also the distinction of being the only coal-pit in Peeblesshire.

In the immediate vicinity of Carlops are certain spots that waken more than a passing interest.

On the North Esk, a few yards above the village, between steep banks, under a canopy of umbrageous trees, and with the romantic adjunct of an old ruined mill in the foreground, there is a waterfall, pleasant to both eye and ear. The cascade consists usually of one broad white shaft of water pouring over a sharp ledge into a deep rocky pool some twelve or fifteen feet below. The roar of the waters can be heard from the bridge, but so snugly is the fall hidden in a nook in the hillside, and so well screened by the foliage of trees, that it cannot be seen except from the rocky bank above the pool on which the ruined mill stands. Locally this ruin is called " Patie's Mill "—Allan Ramsay again—and the rounded height behind it " Patie's Hill." I have frequently heard the song

---

*The round (taking the old road from West Linton) is about 14 miles ; by the new road, 13; by the short-cut through Halmyre Wood, about 12.

of the water-ousel (*cinclus aquaticus*) in the neighbourhood of this fall. It is not unlike the " back-end"
song of the robin. There is a glorious walk up the
North Esk from this point to the Bore Stane, a description of which will be given in a future chapter.

Another place of interest is Charles Wilson's house
and garden, at the south end of the village (Linnburn
Cottage.) Wilson was a plasterer by trade, and his laborious life extended from the middle of the eighteenth
century beyond the first quarter of the nineteenth.
He had a passion for sculpture, and though wholly
untaught in the art he devoted himself to it, feeling
his own way, so to speak, under the impulse of an
instinct which, had it been trained and guided, might
have added to the artistic treasures of the world. He
built at the foot of his garden a little house of strange
design for the bestowal of his smaller sculptures and
curiosities. This is still in existence, and its unusual
appearance inevitably arrests the attention of the
passer-by. His works are remarkable for one in his
position, but they scarcely merit the extravagant
language that has been used regarding them: " He
has erected with his own hands—although unlearned
in the trade—in his little garden, a stone temple of
Gothic architecture which would compare with many
of the famed productions of ancient or modern
Athens."﹒*

---

* From a memorial presented to the Highland Society on Wilson's behalf (1824). See Robert Sanderson's book above cited (p. 39), which
contains a chapter on " Reminiscences of Notable Characters connected
with Carlops."

Drummond Young & Watson]   [Edinburgh

THE WATERFALL BY PATIE'S MILL (CARLOPS)

[To face page 52

Behind Wilson's house, and approached by a pathway skirting his garden, lies Carlops Dean, a bit of country whose physical features catch the eye and excite the wonder of the most unobservant. Roughly speaking, it is a flat in a valley, diversified in the most curious way by what I am tempted to call bubbles and squirts, for at a cursory glance the formation of the Dean looks like the petrifaction of a pot of porridge at the boiling point. " It is a trough, nearly straight, about two miles long; its breadth probably averages 150 yards, and its depth varies from 30 feet to 130. Its direction is N.E. and S.W., and its bottom forms everywhere a marsh or wet meadow. A sharp ridge or ' Kaim,' * about 60 feet high, extends for half a mile along the middle of this valley at its east end; it is broken into separate parts by several transverse openings." † This is the prosaic description of science. The trough is known generally as Windy Gowl,‡ the eastern half only being what is called Carlops Dean. Here is another description—less scientific but more informative: " In the middle of the Dean is Dun Kaim, and above it, likewise in the middle of the flat, appears the romantic rocky cone called the Peaked Craig, with Jenny Barry's Cove, a little grotto from whence issues the Carlops Burn, near it at the bottom of the mountain. § On the other (S.E.) side of the Dean is a recess in the bank called Hell's Hole, opposite a number of craggy passages known as the Carlops

---

* *Anglice*, Comb.
† *Geology of Fife and the Lothians.* Charles Maclaren.
‡ *Anglice*, Gully. § Mount Maw.

Snabs." * A little tributary of the Carlops burn comes bounding down the side of Mount Maw towards the mouth of the Dean.† This is the Linn burn, which, on its way to the valley, breaks into a picturesque little series of small cataracts in a narrow gorge between steep banks of porphyry and sandstone. Those who seek a meditative solitude or a sentimental duality will find few more congenial spots for their purpose.

The Dean just described forms the scenery of the following ballad:

LEEZIE.

Whan Leezie was a lassie, O I lo'ed to lead her hame
By the auld, an' roch, an' rutty road that rins aroun' the Kaim ;
An' when the bairn was weary, she wad rest anaith a tree,
An' her winsome voice wad warble, like the yerlane owre the lea:
  " O Jamie, will ye cairry, will ye cairry, cairry me ? "

O happy were the airms that tuik her up, the bonnie wean,
An' set her doon at last upo' her faither's loupin' stane ;
An' blithe the lad that got the kiss she gied me for ma fee,
Wi' her wee haun's aboot ma neck, as, " Jamie, lad," quo' she,
" Tak' that for a' your care o', a' your care o', care o' me ! "

When Leezie was a woman grown, I lo'ed her aye the same ;
But noo a wale o' younger joes she had to lead her hame ;
Ae nicht, by Carlops Linn, I fand her by her lane a-wee,
An' sat me doon aside her wi', " Ma lass, I lo'e but thee !
O Leezie, will ye mairry, will ye mairry, mairry me ? "

Aince mair she loot ma airm about her lissom waist entwine,
An' tuik ma haun' in hers, and turned her bonnie face to mine ;

---

* See Dr W. Chambers' *History of Peeblesshire.*
† For fuller information about Carlops Dean see Brown's *Notes on Pennicuik.*

An' on ma lips I felt a tear come drappin' frae her e'e,
As a last kiss she gied to me, an' " Jamie, lad," quo' she,
" Tak' that, an' think nae mair o', think nae mair o', mair o'
    me ! "

The thocht o' her is aye wi' me ; and whan the breith o' Spring
Waukens the mavis in the woods an' gars the linties sing,
I hearken for her voice, though noo hersel' I canna see :
I hear it in the liltin' o' the yerlane owre the lea,
That seems to say, " O Jamie, will ye cairry, cairry me ? "

I'll think nae mair o' Leezie when ma hairt has ceased to beat,
An' the cauld yird o' Linton has become ma windin'-sheet:
The thocht o' her is aye wi' me, an' shall be till I dee;
Ay, when I think nae mair o' bonnie Leezie it will be
When earth shall see nae mair o', see nae mair o', mair o' me!

CHAPTER VIII

CARLOPS TO WEST LINTON

OUR route now takes us to West Linton, and here again we have the choice between the old road and the new. The man on the bicycle or on the motor-car must perforce take the new road, for the old one is very rough and hilly. The pedestrian, however, will choose the latter, for in spite of its rugged character, and the fact that it is nearly a mile longer, it is infinitely more picturesque. This road was made by a generation that knew not Macadam, and by engineers who gave no thought to the feelings of the horses that would afterwards have been the severest critics of their work if only their " poor, poor dumb mouths " could have spoken. Pre-Macadamite engineers (General Wade included) allowed the roads they constructed to take the shape of the country. They very seldom made either embankments or cuttings. Consequently on this old road, as on others like it, there are hills so frightfully steep that one wonders how a heavy stage-coach, especially when the track was over the axles on snow or mud, ever reached the top. (Perhaps the feat was accomplished on the famous principle enforced on the Rocky Mountains in the pre-railway days: " First-class passengers, keep your

seats! Second-class passengers, get out and walk!
Third-class passengers, get out and shove!") And
as for the descent of these gradients, one understands
both the frequency and the gruesomeness of the ac-
cidents that occurred.

There is but little traffic on this old road now. Carts
belonging to farms in the vicinity are to be met upon
it occasionally. When the shades of evening fall, in the
delightful months that bridge the chasm between
winters, there is a slight increase of traffic of a more
romantic kind, for couples from West Linton and
Carlops, under the spell of " love's young dream,"
find, in its deserted track, opportunities for the
tender confidences, endearments and caresses that
they would not willingly intrude upon the public eye.

Here and there, on the left, the road is sheltered by
thick belts of woodland, whose shade is grateful on a
hot summer day. On the right the land falls abruptly
to the trough described in the last chapter—Windy
Gowl—which beyond Carlops Dean looks like a long
straight sword-cut in the hills between Mount Maw *
and the ridge traversed by the road. This gully is a
kind of funnel that connects the Lyne valley with that
of the North Esk. It takes its name from the alleged
fact that, no matter how still the air may be elsewhere,
there is always a gale blowing through it. It is consequently a trying place to light a pipe in. To the north,
that is to the right, along the greater part of this road

* Mount Maw was formerly called the Carlops Hill, and believed to be
the western end of the range. What was formerly called Turnip Hill,
opposite Patie's Hill, is now known as the Carlops Hill.

the eye is delighted with a fine panorama of mountain scenery, wild without being rugged. Mount Maw, which dominates the landscape here, contains both lead and silver, and there are to be seen on the hillside traces of mining operations, which, however, do not seem to have been very profitable. Lead Law, which the road crosses about two miles from Carlops, also used to be mined for these metals, and remains of the old workings are in the wood on the left-hand side of the road, nearly opposite Stoneypath farm. A fine view is to be had from here of the terraced course of the Lyne Water. From the shoulder of Lead Law the road dips suddenly and steeply towards the Lyne, in semi-darkness, under tall trees whose branches mingle overhead. The water is crossed by a high old-fashioned bridge, on the parapet of which the wanderer will sit and enjoy the quiet beauty of the limpid expanse of water below locally known as the Lasses' Pool. Between steep, rocky and wooded banks the Lyne—which is here no more than what Englishmen would call a brook—murmurs an accompaniment to the song of the birds and the sighing of the wind through the trees. From one side of the bridge one may almost look down the chimneys of Lynedale House, which in a thick mantle of ivy stands on the left bank of the stream, under a heavy canopy of foliage. A pleasant and romantic situation, but not, one might think, entirely free from the prosaic inconvenience of damp. Medwyn House stands high above the right bank, opposite Lynedale, amid a rampart of fine old trees. It was the Bridgehouse Inn before the

new road was made and the iron horse was foaled.
From the other side of the bridge the eye wanders de-
lightedly over a charming little ravine, whose colouring is always beautiful, but is to be seen in its glory
when the late autumn tints are on the trees. A few
hundred yards up this dell, fronting a little waterfall,
are the ruins of a flax mill, which are celebrated in one
of Robert Sanderson's best-known lyrics.*

Another steep hill to climb and we are on the cross-
road that goes southward to West Linton, and northward to the Cauldstane Slap, the walk through which
is one of the great favourites with Pentland enthusiasts.† Though we are bound for West Linton let us
keep the old road a little longer. It goes from this
point to join the Biggar road at Dolphinton, and
skirts for a quarter of a mile or so the pretty little
moorland golf - course of West Linton, which is
nearly a thousand feet above sea-level, and which,
on a clear day, commands a view of the surrounding
country that, in extent and beauty, has few equals in
Scotland. The Muirfoot, Tweedsmuir, Clydesdale and
Pentland hills encircle the horizon, and the play of
light and colour on the hills near and far presents a
scene of constantly-varying beauty, which, along with
the glorious air of this mountain region, gives an unspeakable charm to a round of golf. The course has
only nine holes, skilfully laid out on a narrow strip of

* "The Auld Lint Mill," in *Frae the Lyne Valley*. In the same book
is a poem entitled " Laird Keyden's Last Wish," which alludes to Lynedale. Keyden was laird of Lynedale a century ago, and desired to be buried by the waterside at the foot of his garden. His wish was disregarded.

† See Chap. XV. p. 137.

turf that embroiders the edge of a bog lying between it and undulating wastes of rough country under long grass. There is room for eighteen holes, but there is a lack of money to make them, and perhaps also a lack of sufficient local enterprise.*

A drove road, leading across the south-western end of the Pentlands, breaks away from our present road at a corner of the golf course. This will be described later.† A few hundred yards beyond this point we light upon the ruins of an inn, which must have been a busy place in the days when the blast of the coach-horn was heard in the land. Tradition has it that Robert Burns once stayed a night here; it further records that he wrote an effusion to the address of the landlady. That he stayed here is probable, for the road was the old highway between Edinburgh and Dumfries; that he wrote erotics to the landlady is not impossible, for he was that kind of man; but one cannot rely absolutely on popular tales like this without further evidence. Very little more than the foundations of this old inn remain to remind the world of what was. One can sit amongst these ruins at dusk and call up from the vasty deep the spirits of that bygone time. So strangely vivid are fancies in the gloaming that we hear the blast of the long-silent

* The golf-course was originally laid out, some twenty years ago, by Robert Millar, long schoolmaster in West Linton, dearly loved by his pupils, and highly respected by all who knew him. He was a man whose character commanded the esteem of all, and whose scholarly tastes added both interest and charm to his character. He died in 1909, and a handsome monument has been erected to his memory in West Linton churchyard.

† See p. 149.

horn, the clatter of hoofs, the jingling of harness, the shouts of the ostlers as the lumbering equipage draws up, with much noise and pother, at the door, the hurried orders of the landlord to bustling hand-maidens; we see the white hats and red coats of coachman and guard, the stiff-legged passengers descending, coated and shawled, from their cramped position, and darting into the cosy parlour, where mine host (or his good lady) gives them a hearty, albeit a mercenary welcome, the rapid change of horses and the gathering of stray rustics to watch with lazy interest the stirring sights that hint of unknown wonders in distant cities; finally we hear the hasty summons to the passengers, the hurried chink of coin, the scramble for places, the letting-go of the horses, as the coach is off once more to the cheery tootle of the guard's horn. Away into the darkness of eternal night! The shrill screech of a locomotive in the valley below brings us back to the twentieth century with a jar of the nerves.

A little further on we cross the Westwater * (or Polintarf), a tributary of the Lyne, by an old bridge which bears the date 1620. It looks primitive enough to be much older, and indeed there is a local tradition to the effect that it occupies the position and embodies the materials of an ancient Roman bridge. Its appearance lends credibilty to the tradition. From various points on this road part of the Southern Mass†

* There is another stream of the same name three miles further west, a tributary of the South Medwyn. (See p. 145).

† See p. 12 (*note*).

of the Pentlands is in view, the foreground being filled with the imposing, lion-shaped Mendick Hill, which, standing a little apart from the rest of the mass, and having a bold, clear-cut outline, makes a fine figure in the landscape. The road winds round the base of Mendick, partly through wood, and partly in the open, till Dolphinton station (Caledonian) is reached. The ascent of Mendick, a favourite walk with both residents and visitors in the district, is best made by a path which strikes up the south-western slope from this road about a mile beyond the bridge. A very extensive view is to be had from the top on a clear day.

Retracing our steps from this point, we return by the golf course to the road that leads past Medwyn House to West Linton, where there is much to interest and please the traveller whose object is not so much to see " ferlies " as to " laze " placidly " far from the madding crowd."

The new road from Carlops to West Linton is much less interesting than the old. At the top of the brae leading out of the village, the road to Macbie Hill breaks away to the left by the new curling-pond, where Carlops disports in winter.* It is not much of a pond in the summer. On the right stands a couple of little cottages smothered in honeysuckle and shrubbery, whence, within my memory, the click of the shuttle in the loom could be heard by the passer-by, for the last of the hand-loom weavers of Peeblesshire was at work. The weaver has joined the great majority, and

* Vestiges of the old curling-pond are to be seen in the middle of Carlops Dean.

the loom is as silent as the coach-horn. A mile of open road, with the Muirfoot Hills visible on the left and the smooth slopes of Mount Maw filling the landscape to the right, brings us to Rutherford House, another roadside inn which has been converted, and consequently risen in rank. Beyond this, some few hundred yards off the main road to the left, is a mineral spring, whose curative properties (real or fancied) have procured for it the name of the Heavenly Aqua Well. At Hazley Burn, three-quarters of a mile beyond Rutherford, we cross the ridge of the watershed between the North Esk and the Lyne, whence the road descends by an easy incline to West Linton. Those who pass this way for the first time will not be able to restrain a little gasp of surprise and pleasure (should meteorological conditions be favourable) when a sudden turn of the road opens to their view the broad green plain, as flat as a billiard-table, shut in on all sides by hill and wood, in a corner of which is huddled away the ancient and picturesque village of Linton, where we shall linger for the space of a few chapters to dwell on its features of interest.

CHAPTER IX

WEST LINTON

LINTON—for the geographical prefix is modern, and serves to distinguish the village from one of the same name in East Lothian—must have had a long history, stretching far back into those years when Pict and Roman disputed the possession of the neighbourhood, and perhaps further; but most of that history has been forgotten. Linton-Roderick (or Rutherick) was, from the time of David I. to the Reformation, a vicarage of the Abbey of Kelso, but all that remains of the old pre-Reformation church is used as the burying-ground of the Fergussons of Spittalhaugh. From the same period doubtless dates its erection into a " burgh of regality."* When the inhabitants of Linton sent an address of welcome to the Prince of Orange at the Revolution they described their village as " the Sub-Metropolitan of Tweeddale." Whatever that may

---

* " Burgh of Regality," like " Appanage of Royalty," is a term that perplexes the modern mind. Not being a lawyer I looked up authorities. Result :—" Burghs of Regality were burghs of barony spiritual or temporal, enfranchised by crown charter, with regal or exclusive criminal jurisdiction within their own territories, and thus called *Regalities*. Some of them . . . especially those which were dependent on the greater bishops and abbots, were of high antiquity, and possessed jurisdiction and privilege of trade only distinguishable from those of royal burghs by being more circumscribed in their limits."—*Chambers' Encyclopædia:* Art., " Borough."—Are you wiser? I am not.

mean, it certainly shows that they had no small idea of their own importance. But there is another side to the picture. " The numerosity, paltriness, pride, contempt of industry, and consequent poverty of the Linton lairds, have always been the subjects of amusement and ridicule. It is a standing joke in the county that at one time there were no less than *five-and-forty* of them; and that of these *fifteen* got assistance from the Poors' Fund, or, as it is shortly expressed, there were forty-five Linton lairds, o' which fifteen *were on the box*." *

Though it was in a siding as regards the old coach-road, which passes three-quarters of a mile to the north of it, yet West Linton was by no means isolated from the world. It stood at the centre of a network of drove roads connecting Tweeddale with the Lothians, and also with the Falkirk Tryst. For there was a great cattle and sheep market at Linton until the year 1856, when, Lanark being found a more convenient centre, it was transferred thither. This market was held both on the village green, an expanse of turf on the left bank of the Lyne, and on a knoll on the other side of the water, which is still known as the Cattle Hill. The drove roads still exist, and are the principal rights-of-way across the Muirfoots to the south and the Pentlands to the north, though now one seldom meets flocks and herds thereupon. West Linton, as a village, is compactly built together. It stands at the north-west corner of the broad green plain already mentioned, where the Lyne, emerging

* Brown's *Notes on Pennicuik*, p. 160.

E

from a deep gorge, breaks away from the Pentlands and holds southward to the Tweed, joining it about four miles above Peebles. The gorge, as seen from the bridge on the high-road, consists of a beautiful sweep of tree-fringed meadow-land coming down to the water's edge on the one side, and a steep rocky bank covered with wood on the other. Mr Bedford's photographs " On the Lyne " and " The Haunt of the Water-Ousel " were taken here. Along the top of the east bank, from the new road to the old, winds a picturesque and irregular pathway, whose characteristics are suggested by its name, " The Cat's Walk." A summer sunset viewed from the bridge is a scene not likely to be forgotten.

A few yards southwards of the bridge two famous springs empty themselves into the Lyne almost opposite to each other. They are not marked in any way to attract the attention of the casual passer-by, but they are visible from the south parapet of the bridge. That to the left is locally known as " Rumbling Tam," while the spring opposite is called " St Mungo's Well." The water from both is held in high estimation, particularly the latter. At the old Linton market on the Cattle Hill, glasses of water from these springs were sold: from " Rumbling Tam " at a half-penny each; from " St Mungo's Well " at a penny.

The village consists mainly of one street, running from north to south, in a slight incline, from the Gordon Arms (or Townhead) Hotel to the parish church. Within the last few years villas of various sizes have been built on the roads in the neighbourhood—some the country residences of Edinburgh citizens, and others for the accommodation of summer visitors. In this way the population of the district is likely to grow, for as West Linton has a southern exposure, wholly sheltered by the hills from the north wind, and partially so from the east, the sanatory influences of its situation and climate are bound to become more widely known. In the irregular polygon that stands for the public square there is a clock-tower with a fountain, a recent restoration of the old village cross. Into the eastern face of this is built a much battered and defaced stone effigy of the so-called " Lady Giffard," with the date 1666 cut on her skirt. This is all that now remains of a " lovely specimen of natural genius without the assistance of art, being the entire labour of one Giffard, a small feu-proprietor in Linton, which he erected in 1666, at his sole expense, to perpetuate the memory of his beloved wife and five children. She is represented in a devout posture, on a pedestal, supported with four infants, and a fifth on her head." * These infants have now disappeared; the fifth, which was not in the original plan of the sculpture, is said to have arrived after the family account of the Giffards was thought to be closed. It will be seen from the above that the name " Lady " Giffard is a misnomer; her antiquity has conferred rank upon her. In former days she was simply called Dame Giffard. Her husband was a zealous Covenanter, and his name can be deciphered amongst others carved on the

* *Companion to Armstrong's Map of Tweeddale.* Quoted in Brown's *Notes on Pennicuik.*

soft rock of the Harbour Craig.* Another piece of his
work is let into the wall of a cottage in the main street,
on the site where his house stood; it is what one might
call a family group in stone, a sort of seventeenth-
century ante-type of the modern cabinet photograph,
with a touch of the allegorical in it. More of his work
may be found on the old gravestones in the churchyard. Though this burying-ground is evidently very
old, I have not been able to decipher any monumental
inscription or date earlier than the beginning of the
seventeenth century. In fact, the oldest I have seen is
on stones built into the wall at the western gate on the
outside. Those bear the date 1601, and the one to the
right, which is more detailed than the others, consists of an oblong tablet, carved in relief, with the
thistle and the rose alternately at the four corners,
and in the centre a shield carrying three " bents " of
lint and a St. Andrew's cross, with the letters I and L
inset in the lateral angles, and a star at the base. This
escutcheon was for long locally taken to be the Linton
arms, but it is actually the arms of the Lawsons of
Cairnmuir, whose burying-ground is within the churchyard just behind. The tablet to the left lacks the
thistle and the rose in the upper corners, and the star
under the cross. There is also pointed out here the
tomb of James Oswald of Spittal,† which was originally covered by the marble top of his dining-table.
This, according to local legend, was removed by
unknown hands—a difficult thing to steal, one would
think, but you could steal the parish church in Lin-

* See p. 48.   † See p. 124.

ton on a dark night without fear of detection. I am informed, however, by a trustworthy local authority, that the vanished tombstone was not of marble, but of " blize "—whatever that may be—and that it was gradually thinned by the village children using it as a kind of slide. It broke in two after a long period of this treatment, and the pieces were thrown into the Lyne. The grave lies behind the gable of the cottage that abuts on the eastern wall. In the middle of the church-yard, amongst the green turf, there is a flat grave-stone with two rudely-carved figures on it which look like an attempt to portray Highlanders, and are supposed to represent two brothers, a minister and a physician, who were killed by an adder. The brothers are variously reputed to have come from West Linton, Dunsyre and Peebles. Another explanation is that the figures are allegorical, and stand for the First and the Second Adam. Life is too short to adjudicate between these traditions, but the figures seem to me older than the seventeenth century. Two ancient and rudely-carved stones are also preserved—dating, perhaps, from the twelfth century, but more probably later—one representing a cross and the other a pair of wool-shears. They formed part of the old pre-Reformation church in all likelihood. The present parish church is a modern structure with a graceful spire. Within, the walls, galleries and pulpit are adorned with very chaste panels and traceries in carved wood, the work of the Misses Fergusson of Broomlee. There are two other churches in Linton: the United Free Church—previous to 1900 a United Presbyterian, and

previous to 1847 a Secession church, built in 1737—
stands in the heart of the village, and at the brae-
head, above the Lyne, there is a neat little episcopal
church, known generally as " the English Chaipel."
It is dedicated to St Mungo (or St Kentigern). The
spring alluded to on p. 66 probably accounts for the
name. The village is in the centre of a spider's web of
roads radiating in all directions. There are three good
routes to Edinburgh; the one described in the foregoing pages, which enters the capital by Morningside,
and two others, which enter it by Liberton and New-
ington. Of these two, the former strikes off the high-
road beyond Nine-Mile-Burn, opposite Walstone farm,
and passing the outskirts of Penicuik at Shottstown
goes *via* Glencorse, Straiton and Liberton to the city,
while the latter goes *via* Leadburn, Wester Howgate
and Auchendinny, joining the other about a mile
beyond Glencorse.* Howgate, it may be noted, has a
niche in literature. It is immortalised in Dr John
Brown's well-known work, *Rab and his Friends*, in the
touching story, told with so much sympathy and
delicacy, of James Noble, the carrier, and his wife,
Alison Græme.

There are two splendid roads to Peebles, and, of
course, through Peebles to the south-eastern Borders.
One, the longer, goes *via* Leadburn and Eddleston;
the other, shorter and far more picturesque, down
the Lyne valley. The Lyne is in sight the whole way
until it is lost in the Tweed, four miles above Peebles;
and, besides the natural beauty of the country through

* This route may be varied by going from Leadburn through Penicuik.

which it passes, the road offers objects of historical interest to the curious. There is the old bridge at Romanno,* whose name one naturally but erroneously connects with the Italian filibusters who exploited our island some twenty centuries ago. The mistake is pardonable, seeing that Roman remains abound in the neighbourhood. Records preserve the memory of a desperate gipsy fight near this bridge in 1677, when the Faas and the Shaws, on their way from Haddington, with hostile intent against the Baillies and the Browns, fell out among themselves. The result of the bloodshed was that Robin Shaw was hanged for murder in the Grassmarket of Edinburgh in February 1678. About a mile down the stream, above the knoll where the present parish church of Newlands stands by the ruins of its predecessor, there are strange formations on the hillside, called the Romanno Terraces, the origin of which remains a mystery. They are supposed to be traces of primitive, perhaps Pictish, agriculture. Those who have seen the terraced rice-fields of Asia will be able to conjure up some idea of those formations, but the space between the ribs (so to speak) is very limited.† The country people used to call them the " Deeces," a

---

* From West Linton one has a choice of two routes to Romanno and the Lyne road to Peebles—either by Spittalhaugh and Stony Brae, past Broomlee Station, or by the Westwater ford and Pirndean, the road across the iron bridge near the parish church. " The lands of Romanno belonged to a family bearing that surname which became extinct in the male line about the beginning of the sixteenth century."—David MacRitchie, *Scottish Gypsies under the Stewarts*, p. 108, *note*.

See also Pennicuik.

† There is something of the same kind on Arthur Seat.

name sufficiently descriptive to those who know the meaning of the word.* Personally, I don't think they have any connection with agriculture, but I have neither hypothesis nor theory to submit on the subject.

Some miles further down the valley stand the stately ruins of Drochill Castle, just above the confluence of the Tarth and the Lyne.† This castle, built by the Regent Morton about 1573, was not completed, and never inhabited by its unfortunate owner. Its ruinous condition, like that of many other Scottish historical relics, is due not so much to the edacious operations of time as to the fact that the building was used for many years as a public quarry. Near Lyne village, where the road passes between the quaint old parish church—well worth a visit—and the school, the remains of a large Roman camp are to be seen. Peeblesshire formed part of the Roman province of Valentia for the first four centuries of our era, and the camp here was occupied for nearly forty years (say A.D. 80-117) as a fortified station in connection with the base at Biggar.‡ A mile or two further on Neidpath Castle comes in sight, standing proudly on its grey old crag above " Tweed's silver

* A "deece" is an article of furniture common in Scottish farmhouses —a long wooden form with a panelled back—and its name is probably a rustic corruption of *dais*.

† The Lyne (except in the Spittalhaugh grounds), the Tarth and the Westwater are all open fishings. The prevalence of fishing by illegal methods is spoiling all three streams. There is need not only for the close time recently—and not too soon—decreed by Parliament, but also for an enactment making the sale of trout illegal. This would choke off those who fish for gain, not or sport.

‡ See Chambers' *History of Peeblesshire*.

THE HAUNT OF THE WATER-OUZEL (LYNE VALLEY)
(From a Photograph kindly sent by Mr E. J. Bedford, Eastbourne)

[To face page 72.

stream." This is one of the chain of strongholds, extending from east to west near the Borders, erected by our suffering ancestry to restrain the lawless ambitions of Southern "pock-puddens." *Peebles is a mile beyond this. To the south-west from Linton two roads are available to Biggar, ten miles away; one *vià* Blyth Bridge and Skirling, † and the other the highroad, which must still be our route for a few miles in our journey round the Pentlands.

Another fine road, rather steep in parts, goes *vià* Blyth Bridge to Broughton, thence over the Tweedsmuir Hills to the Talla reservoir, and past the Devil's Beef Tub to Moffat and Annandale. Besides these main-roads there are innumerable cross-roads and tracks connecting them in various directions; many of these are rideable, offering to cyclists a large choice of circular tours. To pedestrians they offer a still more varied choice.

The Lyne valley has long been a happy huntingground for antiquarians. There are interesting Pictish and Roman remains—camps, burial *tumuli* containing stone coffins, etc. A Pictish fort—locally believed to be Roman—stands on a hill-top behind the parish church manse. The site is marked by a rectangular

---

*A very pleasant round can be made by taking this road from Linton to Peebles (14½ miles), thence to Leadburn *vià* Eddleston (11 miles), and thence to Linton again *vià* Lamancha and Spittalhaugh (8 miles). Cyclists can shorten the journey to 22½ miles and economise their strength by taking the train from Peebles to Leadburn. This shortened cycle-ride is extremely pleasant, both on account of the pretty country traversed and the fact that the road is on the down-grade most of the way.

† Leaving Linton, take the road by Westwater ford and Pirndean (*see* p. 71, *note*)

enclosure of stones, within which are three scraggy trees, and it affords a wonderfully extensive view of the surrounding district. Flint arrow-heads have been turned up by the plough on the northern slope of this hill.

Even to the most unscientific and uninstructed eye, the plain in which West Linton stands is the bed of an old lake that has only recently disappeared, and must have covered an area of nearly fifteen square miles. (I use the word " recently " in its geological sense, of course.) I picture it stretching from Whitefield to Newlands, with perhaps a waterfall in the neighbourhood of the Romanno Terraces: between Whitefield and West Linton the plain is familiarly called The Bog, which name is preserved for the enlightenment of posterity in the poetical and euphonious Bog's Bank Road, which runs from the parish church of Linton to the Westwater ford. Often in the early morning, or late evening, one can see a pall of white mist covering the greater part of the plain while the surrounding country is clear. Looking across the valley from the Edinburgh road above the village (from which the best view of the plain is to be had), one needs little imagination to fill the landscape with a noble sheet of water. It is noteworthy that all the traces of Roman and Pictish military operations are above the level of this hypothetical lake, and also— though I am not quite sure of this—most of the ancient graves that have been discovered. The soil of the plain is alluvial, crossed by a bank of conglomerate between Broomlee and Spittalhaugh. All which evidences seem to point to the fact that the waters have only recently disappeared from the face of the earth in this quarter. Indeed, some of the older inhabitants declare that, within their memory, before modern systems of drainage were introduced, when the Lyne and its tributaries were in heavy flood, the whole plain lay under water for several days at a time.

There is a legend to the effect that the late Queen Victoria, when she contemplated the purchase of a country retreat in Scotland, had laid before her proposals as to two desirable spots: one was Balmoral, which she ultimately chose; the other, West Linton. She perhaps chose wisely—for Scotland—because, though the climatic conditions of both districts are nearly equal, her choice of Balmoral took her further into the heart of Scotland, to a spot where Highlands and Lowlands meet, and where she endeared herself by her simple, kindly life to both Gael and Saxon.

Note.—While these sheets were passing through the press (Feb. 1910) two of the trees on the Pictish fort (p. 74), were blown down by a furious gale.

CHAPTER X

WEST LINTON TO DOLPHINTON, DUNSYRE AND CARNWATH

PURSUING our leisurely tramp round the Pentlands, we take the high-road to Dolphinton *en route* for Dunsyre and Carnwath. There are other ways of getting to these two places over the hills, and these will be described in a subsequent chapter. Meanwhile we keep the Biggar road, and about a mile on our way we pass the pretty little loch of Slipperfield, one of the few surviving lochs of Peeblesshire, a photograph of which, by Mr Bedford, is reproduced here. I say " surviving lochs," because the conformation of the country shows that large tracts of the county were under water at one time, at a period not geologically remote. There are several extensive bogs or mosses, which even a tyro in geology can see to be the dregs, so to speak, of ancient lakes. Slipperfield Loch is little more than a large pond. It is shut in by a thick wall of pine and fir; it is a haunt of tame swans and some common wildfowl, and in winter it is a favourite resort of the curlers in the neighbourhood; but owing to its sheltered position it needs a long and hard frost to bring it into proper condition for the devotees of the roaring game.

Further on, a few hundred yards on the left of the

SLIPPERFIELD LOCH AND MENDICK HILL.

(From a Photograph kindly sent by Mr E. J. Bedford, Eastbourne)

[To face page 76

road, lies the White Moss, a considerable expanse of
bog, which is a famous breeding-place for the black-
headed gull (*Larus ridibundus*). These birds, locally
named " picternies," haunt the moss in myriads; and
to walk across the bog in nesting-time—April and
May—is to fill the sky with vociferous clouds of gulls,
whose screams are deafening, and whose wild evolu-
tions overhead make one think he is in the midst of a
Brobdingnagian snowstorm. Recently some hen-caper-
cailzies (*Tetrao urogallus*) have been seen on this moss,
one by myself.* On the right-hand side of the road are
what may be called the outworks of Mendick Hill,
and, for a considerable distance, an irregular row of
what seem to be sandhills covered with turf. The road
itself is bleak and dreary, but the view in front, if the
landscape be clear, amply compensates for that.
Facing us is the sombre outline of the Black Hill
above Dolphinton (1689 ft.), which, though near the
Pentlands, is not of them; while to the left of that
the horizon is closed in by hills of the Tweedsmuir and
Tinto ranges. A sunset in early spring or late autumn
over these hills exhibits dioramic effects of extraordinary beauty. About three miles from West Linton
the two railway termini of Dolphinton are reached.
This sounds imposing, but as the termini are two forlorn little shanties on opposite sides of the high-road,

---

* This bird, once very common in Scotland, was extinct for a period,
until 1837, when a few pairs were imported from Scandinavia and let
loose in the neighbourhood of Crieff. It has spread slowly since then into
Forfarshire and Stirlingshire. Some ornithologists maintain that the hen-
bird is the pioneer of new colonies, and that while on the pioneering expedition she mates freely with the black-cock (*Tetrao tetrix*).

the imposingness looks a bit of an imposition. The one is the terminus of a little branch of the North British Railway's branch line to Peebles. (The frivolous may call it a twig.) The other is a Caledonian branch from Carstairs. Why a hamlet of half a dozen houses should have two rival stations puzzles the casual visitor, but the existing situation is the result of a Parliamentary compromise between the rival companies, both of which, for reasons that are not obvious to the uninitiated, were extremely anxious to get to Dolphinton. Now that they have both got there, they do not seem to have made much of it. The real reason of this wasteful rivalry seems to have been that the North British were very anxious to get into Lanarkshire, and the Caledonian were equally anxious to keep them out. At present, in Dolphinton, they are like the pickets of opposing armies, who fraternise and exchange flasks till the battle begins.

Just beyond the railway stands a sharp conical hill of turf-covered sand. Its name is Keppat Hill, but it is locally known as " The De'il's Riddlin's." In this latter name there is a popular explanation of its origin which is contemptuously rejected by men of science, who, as is well known, are dreadful sceptics. (*Riddle*, it may be remarked, is the Scotch word for *sieve*.) The story goes that, at a date not mentioned, the Devil stood on this spot with a sieve in his hand, into which a man standing on the opposite hillside—Ingraston Hill—flung rocks and soil with a long-shafted shovel. The Devil carefully sifted out the sand and flung the rocks into Biggar Moss, some six or seven

Drummond Young & Watson]

DOLPHINTON CHURCH

[*Edinburgh*

[*To face page* 78

miles away. His object in doing so is not stated. Confirmation of the legend is afforded by two sandy holes, one on each side of the grass-grown slope, distantly resembling gigantic footprints, which are alleged to mark the exact spot where His Brimstone Majesty stood on this interesting occasion. The prints are those of a flat-footed person, and the orthodox belief is that the Devil, when visiting the haunts of men, always sports the cloven hoof.*

Dolphinton lies on the watershed between the Tweed and the Clyde. We cross the Garvald burn † between the railway and the village, and that is the last of the streams making for the Tweed as we go westward. And here we leave the white roads of Peeblesshire for the red roads of Lanarkshire, the burn being at this point the boundary between the two counties. Passing a row of cottages, which constitutes the main mass of the hamlet, we reach the parish church, one of the smallest in Scotland, yet one whose antiquity and quaintness compel the most careless passer-by to stop and to look about him. The wee kirk crowns a low green knoll on the right, and all around, "where heaves the turf in many a mouldering heap," at every imaginable angle, stand the old grey, lichen-covered stones that mark the graves

* This mound is one of the *Kames* described by Sir Archibald Geikie in *The Scenery of Scotland*, who hints its connection with the mythology that has crystallised round the name of Michael Scott, the wizard. The local legend, however, enjoys an equal probability.

† The name is derived (according to Dr W. Chambers) from the ancient British *garw*, "violent," and *alt*, "a stream." The burn is not, however, more violent than ordinary streams.

where " the rude forefathers of the hamlet sleep." The most interesting grave is that of Major Learmont, who fought at the battle of Rullion Green,* and who, having survived both it and the consequent persecution, died at an advanced age, an elder in Dolphinton church. A flat stone near the kirk door marks his resting-place. We now turn to the right and make our way round the north-eastern base of the Black Hill, along a pleasant road sheltered by trees, and somewhat hilly. Not far from the church, in a slope of the Black Hill to the left, the remains of an old Roman camp are to be seen. Dolphinton † House and its prettily-wooded policies fill the hollow below. The first road we pass on the right, at Roberton, leads to Garvald House and to Dolphinton station; the second carries us across the South Medwyn valley towards Dunsyre, and as we make our way thither we have in front of us a fine panorama of mountain scenery, in the foreground of which is the bold and abrupt peak of Dunsyre Hill (1313 feet), a mass of intrusive dolerite,‡ and behind it the softer outline of the Mid Hill (1347 ft.). Dunsyre is a picturesque village snuggling close under its guardian hill. Though a railway passes through the parish, it is still very primitive, having no house for the refreshment of man or beast. Many a hungry and thirsty pedestrian has suffered grievous disappointment there. As at Dol-

* See p. 27, *et seq.*

† The name Dolphinton is said to be derived from Coss Dolfain, brother of Coss Patrick, first Earl of Dunbar, about the beginning of the twelfth century. See the *New Statistical Account*.

‡ The cliffs are called " The Corbies' Craigs."

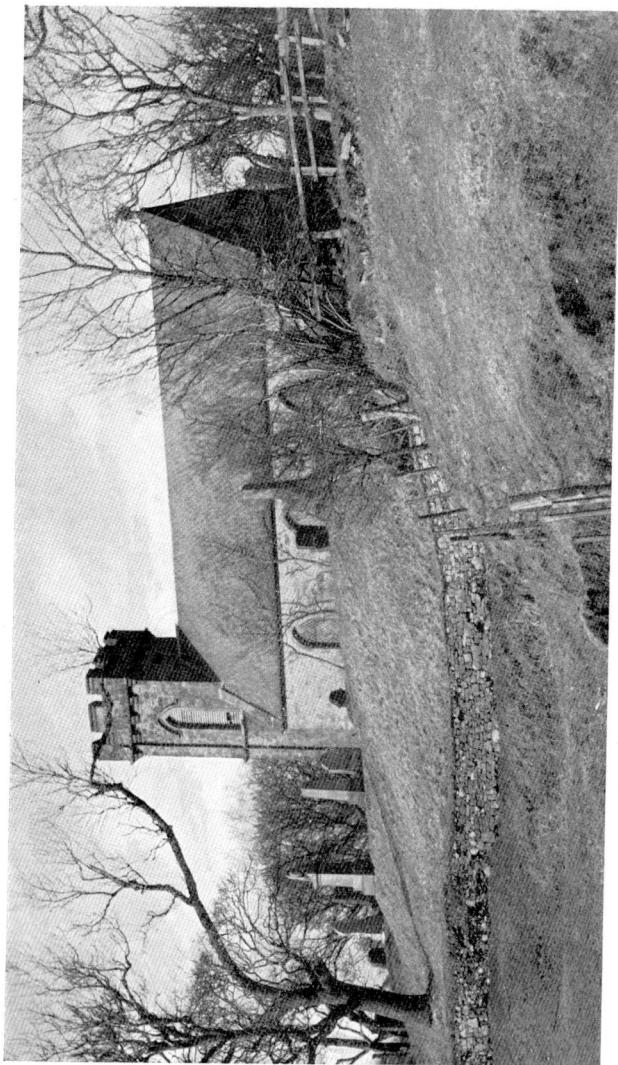

Drummond Young & Watson]

DUNSYRE CHURCH

[Edinburgh

[To face page 80

phinton, so here, the chief centre of interest is the
parish church, which, with its square tower and its
broad roof, standing on a knoll amid a grove of tombstones, has the quaint look that many country
churches have, of a hen gathering her chickens under
her wings. The old bell in the tower, which still calls
the faithful to prayer, but has lost all its music through
the wear and tear of time, bears the date of 1568.
Outside the north wall of the church, framed and
glazed for its protection, is one of the few remaining
specimens of the " jougs," an iron collar fastened to
the wall by a chain, an instrument that was used for
the pillorying of offenders in the brave days of old.
Associated with the " jougs " there was often another
instrument of correction and torture, called the
" branks," an iron bridle and gag combined, which
was fitted to the headpiece and mouth of ladies ad-
dicted to violent and abusive language. Some op-
pressed Scottish husbands have been known to voice
their regret that this tranquillising device has fallen
into disuse in these degenerate times.*

* I have had the privilege of perusing some of the old Session-records
of the church, which are preserved in the manse. Very quaint and amus-
ing some of these records are, yet they bear a striking testimony to the
assiduity and faithfulness with which minister and elders discharged their
duties. I was permitted by the present minister—Rev. W. Smith, M.A.—
to make the following curious extract :—

" 1702 . . . . . . Compeared David Niven and was Interrogat qdr or
not he vented these following principles 1mo that yr are more saved than
damned 2ndo that fast dayes had not warant from Scripture 3tio that he
thought it not peoples duty to love yr enemies 4to that a Lie is approven
from the word of God 5to that heathen may be saved without the knowledge of Jesus Christ 6to that Magick is ane airt yt may be studied, and
he doubts not but all learned men did study it, and counts it no sin to

F

Dunsyre has a place in Covenanting memories. Donald Cargill, the " outed " minister of the Barony Church in Glasgow, who, with the stricter Covenanters, protested against the restoration of Charles II., who fought at Bothwell Brig, who was art and part with Richard Cameron in the Sanquhar Declaration, and the hero (or villain, according to the reader's sympathies) of the Torwood Excommunication (1680), preached his last sermon on the village common. He was arrested that same night at Covington Mill,* carried first to Lanark, and then to Edinburgh, where he was tried and executed in July 1681. According to Dr Burns, the learned editor of Woodrow's *History of the Sufferings of the Church of Scotland*, Cargill expounded Jeremiah i. and then preached on Isaiah xxvi. 20, 21: " Come, my people, enter thou into thy chambers, and shut thy doors about thee: hide thyself as it were for a little moment, until the indignation be overpast. For, behold, the Lord cometh out of

Learn it if it was not immediately from the devil but from books 7timo that people may win to heaven qdr God will or not."

The culprit admitted that he had "vented" these principles as much for discussion as through conviction. The leaf containing the upshot of this heresy case is unfortunately missing.

The spelling and punctuation of the above transcript are not mine.

The oldest gravestone in the churchyard seems to be that of one Mr Somerville, minister of the parish, who died in 1646. Mr Somerville was a " black prelatist," and seems to have lived in terror of his life, owing especially to the threats of a zealous Presbyterian named Baillie of Todhills. The Marquis of Douglas extended protection to the minister, but when that nobleman went to the wars, Mr Somerville, fearing an attack from Baillie, took to the hills for some days, and lived near a spring on the hill-side which is still called "the Curate's Well." The records of this curious case are preserved in the archives of the Presbytery of Lanark.

* Covington is near Thankerton, to the north of Tinto Hill.

His place to punish the inhabitants of the earth for their iniquity: the earth also shall disclose her blood, and shall no more cover her slain." * Cargill, like Peden and others of his time, was popularly believed, and probably believed himself, to be an inspired prophet.

The district in early times must have been much more populous than it is now, for traces of ancient fortalices abound in the neighbourhood, and tradition points to various sites where some that have left no trace are said to have stood. It bears marks also of the Roman occupation. " The line by which the army of Agricola reached the camp at Cleghorn lies through the parish of Dunsyre, and the road can be traced up the county of Tweeddale.† The entrance to the glen, or valley, where Dunsyre is situated, is called the Garvald or Garrel; which remains the most easy and natural communication between the east and west of the plain. Through this rugged pass lies the Roman line, marked out by a dyke of earth." ‡

To the north-east of Dunsyre there is a very fine rising stretch of moorland running into the heart of the Pentlands, whence views at once extensive and enchanting can be had of the surrounding country. § Enjoying a lazy summer day at full length on the heather, thoroughly comfortable, wholly receptive or

* Woodrow's *History*, edited by Dr Robert Burns (1829), vol. iii. p. 279, *note*.

† *i.e.* Peeblesshire.

‡ *New Statistical Account* (1845), Parish of Dunsyre.

§ Some of the hill walks yet to be described cross this moor in various directions.

languidly meditative, one envies neither kings nor millionaires.

To the south-west lies the broad alluvial plain watered by the South Medwyn, a stream held in repute by anglers, though not what it once was. In spite of various Acts of Parliament to prevent the utter extinction of the trout in the open waters of Scotland, there is need for a modern Isaiah to proclaim, " They that spread nets upon the waters shall languish "— in jail, for preference.

Leaving Dunsyre we take the road over the hill to Newbigging.* The road is rather rough and steep in places, but it presents little difficulty to the cyclist, and none at all to the pedestrian. We are here approaching the end of the Pentlands, the hills becoming lower and flatter as we proceed, gradually sinking into a slightly undulating plain of bleak moorland. Newbigging is a little triangular village on the road between Glasgow and Peebles. Its name is locally pronounced " Neebicken " (with the accent on the first syllable), which is likely to have been its original designation. The one point of interest to the casual visitor—apart from the quiet charm of a country hamlet—is the cross.† Concerning which a native

* Another route from Dolphinton to Newbigging may be taken. Passing Dolphinton Church keep to the Biggar road as far as Melbourne farm, then take the cross-road to the right, which leads through the village of Elsrickle (Elsridgehill), past the Roman camp at Borelands (on the left) to Newbigging railway station. It may be said that the whole district described in this chapter—not the least picturesque or interesting in the county—is ignored by Black's *Guide to Scotland*.

† This is not visible from the Glasgow-Peebles road. To see it one has to turn up the road leading to Dunsyre.

Drummond Young & Watson]

THE CROSS AT NEWBIGGING

[To face page 84

gave me the following account: I cannot vouch for its accuracy, having found no confirmation of it elsewhere. Skirling Fair, my informant said, used to be held at Burn Grange,* some three miles to the north of the village, and the cross now in Newbigging stood in the middle of the market area there. When the fairs ceased to be held at Burn Grange, the inhabitants of Skirling laid claim to the cross, and sent a body of men to transport it to their own village. The Newbigging weavers, however, got wind of this scheme, lay in wait for the Skirling boys, and, after a fierce fight, robbed them of the cross and set it up as spuilzie where it now stands.

The distance from Newbigging to Carnwath is about two and a half miles; the road crosses the North Medwyn about half-way, and then passes a hamlet called Kaimend,† whose name indicates that it marks the end of the Pentland range.

Carnwath is a considerable village, which deserves to be better known both by the outside world and by its own inhabitants. It consists mainly of a long steep street, running from east to west, and its name is said to mean the cairn of the ford, the cairn being the moat described below. I am not satisfied with this explanation, but have no other to offer. Half-way down the main street stands the old jail, with its

---

* Burn Grange is near the confluence of the Sala burn with the Westruther burn, one of the main tributaries of the North Medwyn. Newbigging stands above the point at which the valleys of the two Medwyns join. The waters meet about two miles to the westward, shortly before they disappear in the Clyde.

† *i.e.* Comb end, or end of the ridge.

crow-stepped gable, and beside it the market-cross. At the west end of the village, where the road descends towards a thick grove of trees, stands the parish church. The present edifice was built in 1798, on the site of an ancient pre-Reformation church, founded in 1386, and alongside of St Mary's aisle, a very fine old chapel, dating from 1424, with an exquisitely beautiful window of stained glass, framed in stone after the later decorated style, facing the north.

To the north-west of the village, in a fine stretch of meadow-land, there is a large plum-pudding-shaped earthen mound, fenced in and covered with trees, called the Moat, the meaning and purpose of which have been entirely forgotten by the inhabitants of the district. In several flying visits to Carnwath, I tried to get some account of it from the inhabitants, but was unsuccessful. A mile to the northward of the Moat, across the Carnwath Moss, lie ruins so very ruinous that they do little more than mark the site of the ancient Couthally * Castle. With regard to the Moat, the *New Statistical Account* says: " The Sommerville papers mention this mound as a memorial of the first Baron Sommerville's adherence to the ' Brucean interest,' in opposition to the ' Balliol

---

* King James VI., when guest at this castle, suggested that its name should be "Coodaily," because for the sustenance of His Majesty and retinue one cow and twenty sheep were slaughtered every day. The castle has a place in the legend on which is founded Sir Walter Scott's ballad, *The Gray Brother*, the tragedy of Margaret Heron. This legend is given in detail by Miss Margaret Warrender in *Walks near Edinburgh*. Miss Warrender quotes other passages from the *Memorie of the Somervilles* bearing on Couthally.

faction.' Thus, after stating that ' during all the days of his life he was a constant adherent of King Robert Bruce, and ane adherer to his sone King David's interest when it was in the most desperate condition,' they thus proceed: ' Witnes his casting up a quantitie of earth, of his lands upon the south-west * of Carnwath toune, which, makeing a little hill, 'tis called yet *omnis terra*. This was the custom of these tymes, by which homage they that held the King of Scotland supreme under God were distinguished from the Balliol party, or such as owed any homage to the King of England.' " † Some seem to think that the mound was built for the defence of Couthally Castle, but my opinion is that the Moat was the predecessor of the castle. In King David's time, Scotland was divided into baronies after the Norman fashion, and in the centre of each barony, for purposes both defensive and juridical, there was built a mound with a stockade on the top, after a pattern which may be seen on the Bayeux tapestry. The stone and lime castles were of a later date, and were erected in the neighbourhood of the mounds. There is a moat at Annan of the same type as this at Carnwath, and there is a popular belief that the old parish church of Annan occupies the site of a castle that has long since disappeared. Hence it would seem that the moats were better able to survive the ravages of time and war than the masonry of the keeps.

Carnwath has long been associated with the Lock-

---

* (*Sic*). It should be, however, "north-west."
† *New Statistical Account*, Parish of Carnwath

harts of Lee * and Coutland; it gave also the title of earl to the Dalzell family in 1639. History has preserved the name and the deeds of the famous Earl of Carnwath, who was "out" in the Jacobite rising of 1715. The Lockharts of Lee hold their Carnwath property on condition of maintaining an annual foot-race in the village. This race—called "the Red Hose Race," from the pair of red stockings and the accompanying guinea competed for—is regularly held about the middle of August in connection with a sheep and horse market and various athletic games. Farmers used to tilt with wooden lances at a ring on the green, the prize being a gold finger-ring. The " Red Hose " is the red-letter day of the year for the village, and stalls with gingerbread, sweets and other commodities line the street. Travelling shows of all kinds add to the local excitement.

Within the memory of a few still living the town-drummer used to go round the streets at 5 a.m. waking the inhabitants to get their cattle out. The town-herd followed him and drove the cattle to the common pasture.† As I have said, Carnwath deserves to be better known. Its history and antiquities will bear more investigation than they have yet received, and

* Lee House is in the neighbourhood of Lanark. The reader is referred to the introduction to Sir Walter Scott's *Talisman*, a story which is founded on the " Lee-penny," the famous charm which is an heirloom in the Lockhart family.

† Mr Wm. Young writes :—" Some of the lazy folk got him (the drummer) to tap on the window with his drumstick. The cows going through the village to pasture was an interesting sight. The herd began at the head of the town, and cow after cow joined the gang. On their return, to see each cow leave the herd at its own byre was very pretty."

Drummond Young & Watson]   [*Edinburgh*

COURT-HOUSE, JAIL, AND CROSS, CARNWATH

[*To face page* 88.

will well repay labour spent thereon. A golf-course has recently been opened to the west of the town, and that is likely to prove an attraction to those who " act in the living present," who " let the dead past bury its dead," and let the future look out for itself. The village is a good centre for visiting many interesting spots. There are several inns in the place, but the accommodation is limited.

CHAPTER XI

WE now turn our faces towards Edinburgh, and take the road which skirts the north side of the Pentland range. In itself it is not a very interesting road, but from several points in its course there are paths (rights-of-way and otherwise) leading into the wilder regions of the hills, each of which in turn the man on whom the Pentlands have laid their spell will dutifully explore. Some of these will be described further on. I have walked and ridden this road many times, under various conditions, favourable and the reverse, but the memory of the awful day when I pushed a disabled bicycle for fifteen miles, in the teeth of a furious hurricane, colours all my impressions of it. It is bleak, it is lonely, it is fatiguing, whether you are afoot or awheel, and one can scarcely conceive that within a few miles of the capital there could be such a wilderness as the region traversed by it. But the Pentlands, rising grandly above the great wastes of moorland on the right, with their clear-cut outline and their sombre shadows, keep the eye engaged, and shorten the weary miles.

We have to go nearly three miles from Carnwath before we reach the Pentland area proper, which may

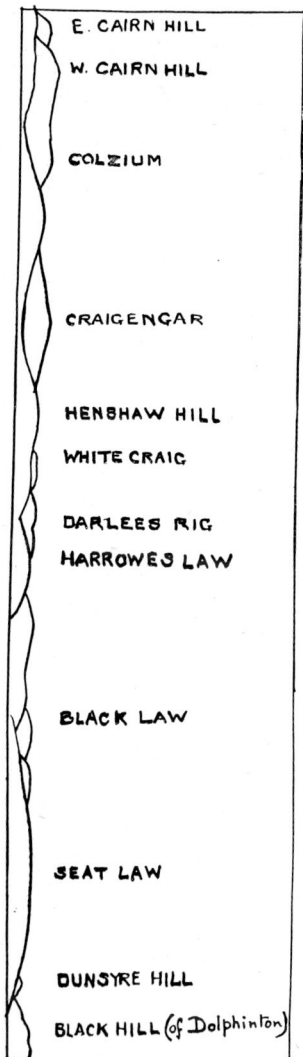

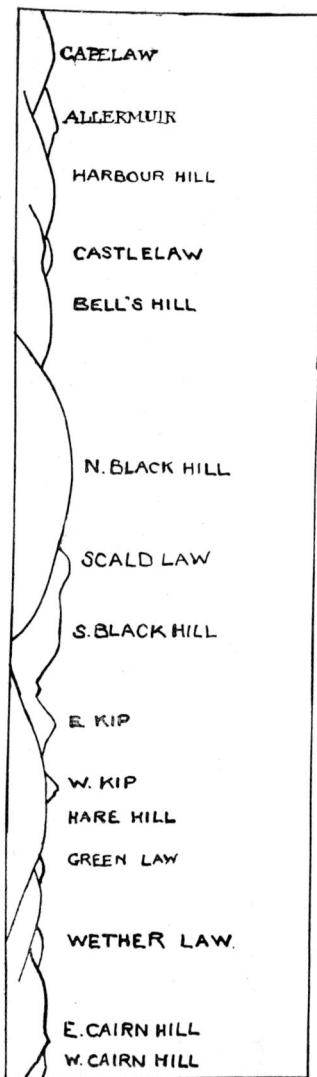

A. **South Mass from Auchengray**

A.	B.
E. CAIRN HILL	CAPELAW
W. CAIRN HILL	ALLERMUIR
	HARBOUR HILL
COLZIUM	
	CASTLELAW
	BELL'S HILL
CRAIGENGAR	
	N. BLACK HILL
HENSHAW HILL	
WHITE CRAIG	SCALD LAW
DARLEES RIG	S. BLACK HILL
HARROWES LAW	
	E. KIP
BLACK LAW	W. KIP
	HARE HILL
	GREEN LAW
SEAT LAW	WETHER LAW.
DUNSYRE HILL	E. CAIRN HILL
BLACK HILL (of Dolphinton)	W. CAIRN HILL

A.—South Mass from Auchengray
B.—The Hills from Marchbank (Balerno)

[To face page 90

be said to begin at Redford bridge, where the road crosses the North Medwyn.* Here begins, and continues for twelve miles, the dreary stretch of road popularly called the " Lang Whang." Half a mile before Redford bridge, to the right, there is access to the Wauk Mill and to Burn Grange, which in days bygone subtended a larger angle to local importance than they do now. The first view of the Pentlands at this point is rather unimpressive—a series of low sandstone hills under a carpet of dark-coloured heather. The surface of the road is immaterial to the pedestrian, but the cyclist wonders why the Lanark County Council has substituted for the old-fashioned blue road-metal, which, when rolled, was like a cement pavement, a top-dressing of pounded bricks and tiles, unrolled. I don't say this is the material used, but it looks as if it were. Indeed, one is tempted to believe that the Council has bought dirt cheap, in the interests of economy, and emptied at haphazard, a few cartloads of discarded Glasgow chimney-cans. I don't think the road has ever seen a steam-roller. One hopes better things of the Midlothian County Council, till he passes above Tarbrax at the Maidenwellbrow, the county boundary, where, in the valley below, tall brick stalks vomit black clouds of smoke and a foul oily smell. But the hope is disappointed, for Midlothian throws down chopped slates instead of Lanark's pounded chimney-cans, and leaves the scattered

* An easier road for the cyclist branches off to the left opposite Kerse-well House, a mile and a half from Carnwath, and goes to Edinburgh *via* Auchengray and Midcalder.

heaps thereof unrolled, to be trodden down by what traffic passes along the road. The cyclist suffers accordingly, and breathes the fervent prayer that in the next world the county councillors may be compelled, in a torrid climate, to cycle for a millennium over the roads they have made. The " Lang Whang," part of the high-road between Edinburgh and Lanark, is one of the worst in the country, and does little credit to the authorities. The chief scenic interest of the road begins when Craigengar and the two Cairn Hills heave in sight. All the rest of the way the Pentland range stretches like a great rampart on the south. Its contours are not so imposing as when seen from the other side, the slopes to the north being more gradual, as a rule, but the general colouring is more sombre in tone. On a clear winter afternoon, with the outline of the ridge sharply cut against an opaline sky, the rich deep purples and blues of the hills, above the misty grey-green of the intervening moors, present a picture which the painter's fingers itch to reproduce, but which at the same time reminds him of the limitations of his art.

Four and a half miles from Carnwath, opposite Boston Cottage, an old stage-house now in ruins, is the drove road leading across the hills to West Linton *viâ* Medwynhead, with a branch going to Dunsyre.* Rather more than two miles beyond this, half a mile short of Maidenwellbrow, another path strikes across the range by Henshaw Hill and the Garval Syke to Dunsyre, Dolphinton and West Linton.† Two

* See p. 156. † See p. 151.

miles further on, close by the Crosswood reservoir,* another path makes for Henshaw Hill, where it joins the one last mentioned.

Another two miles, and in the valley below the Water of Leith may be descried, which henceforth accompanies our road, more or less closely, till we reach the neighbourhood of Edinburgh. Below the little village of West Causewayend lies the Harper Rig reservoir,† at the south corner of which stand the ruins of Cairns Castle, said to have been founded by the famous Chancellor Crichton about the middle of the fifteenth century. A cross-road to the right, at the village school, leads down to these ruins. Harper Rig preserves the old name of the East Cairn Hill, which was long supposed to be the highest point of the range. Modern scientific measurements have reduced it to the fourth place. The road now passes high above the reservoir, over the toilsome shoulder of Auchinoon Hill, and then down to the old toll-house, whence one of the best known of the trans-Pentland paths strikes away to the right, past the east end of the reservoir to the Cauldstane Slap between the Cairn Hills, and down the Lyne valley to West Linton.‡ Half a mile further on the ruins of Little Vantage inn (on the right) awake a passing interest. Over two miles further a path goes southward by Haugh Head farm to another pass in the Pentlands by the Bore Stane, between East Cairn

* The Crosswood reservoir is a compensation pond in connection with the Edinburgh Water Trust, completed in 1869.

† This reservoir is also a compensation pond in connection with Edinburgh and District Water Works. It dates from 1859.

‡ See p. 137.

Hill and Cock Rig by the North Esk valley to Carlops,* a branch of which goes by Todholes to Bavelaw Castle,† there joining other paths, which cross the hills in various directions. From Auchinoon to Edinburgh the road is well cared for, and has a good surface; it is also downhill, and therefore easy both to the foot-passenger and the wheelman. The country now loses its bleak aspect; the land is well cultivated, woods and plantations relieve the monotony of the land-scape, and when Balerno station is reached we are practically out of the Pentland area, and back to populous civilisation again.‡ Our present route does not take us through Balerno village, which lies half a mile to the south of the railway station. The road to the right, which leads to the village, leads also across the hills in two directions, one by Bavelaw Castle § and the other by Harelaw ‖; but we keep straight on to-wards the village of Currie on the left side of the pretty ravine through which the Water of Leith makes its way seawards.¶

Half-way to Currie, on the opposite side of the ravine, may be seen the ivy-draped ruins of Lennox Tower, associated with the memory of the Earl of Lennox, father-in-law of Mary Queen of Scots, of Lord Darnley, his son, of the Regent Morton, and of

* See p. 127.   † See p. 115.

‡ It is somewhat trying to travellers in these regions that there is no house of call for man or beast between Carnwath and Balerno, a distance of 18 miles. Men on the tramp here need a good square meal, and they cannot get it unless they carry it with them.

§ See p. 115.   ‖ See p. 99.

¶ The Caledonian Railway from Balerno to Edinburgh is here available

James VI. Tradition says that an underground passage connected this building with Colinton Tower, three miles away, and there is the usual legend of the adventurous piper who went along the passage in a later age playing gaily on his pipes till he was choked by the foul air. The same legend is attached to every place in Scotland where tradition speaks of an underground passage. The mortality of pipers in a bygone inquisitive age must therefore have been tremendous.

Currie is a very old village, and in its neighbourhood stand many houses of great historical interest. At the entrance to the village a road goes to the right, crossing the Water of Leith by an ancient bridge which dates from the fourteenth century, and whose sombre aspect has passed into a proverb (" Dark as Currie Brig "), and making for the Pentlands past the Malleny shooting-range and the Maiden's Cleugh to the Glencorse valley. This, it may be remarked, was the route taken by General Dalzell and his dragoons in pursuit of the Covenanters to the fatal field of Rullion Green.* Meanwhile we go no farther than the old parish church, which, like so many other country churches, stands in a grove of tombstones on a low green knoll on the side of the ravine. There is one stone of special interest in this churchyard, the tomb of a Knight Templar. It lies near the east side of the church, and upon it there can be traced a sword, and the eight-pointed cross of the Knights Templar, surmounted by a rosary. The famous order of the Templars had an establishment close by, on the river side,

* See p. 29.

the memory of which is enshrined in the name Kin-leith (*i.e.*, Kil-Leith), or Chapel of Leith. From Currie we go on to Colinton, passing through Juniper Green, a village which is being rapidly annexed, and its rustic characteristics destroyed, by Edinburgh villa-dom. The heights of the North Mass of the Pentlands are in view most of the way on the right, and the Water of Leith keeps close to the roadside, with the railway between. One is struck by the number of ruined houses and mills along this valley, and is tempted to believe that the long-expected German invasion of Scotland has actually taken place, and has been conducted with the anticipated Teutonic ferocity.

Colinton is steeply built on the two sides of the ravine at the head of the delightful gully called Colin-ton Dell, where rock, stream and wood combine to make a scene of exquisite beauty. Readers are re-ferred to Robert Louis Stevenson's *Memories and Portraits* * for a charming description of the neigh-bourhood. Stevenson's maternal grandfather, Dr Balfour, was parish minister of Colinton for many years, and his famous grandson has immortalised a spot which is rapidly changing its character, for like Juniper Green, it is suffering from the invasion of villadom, which, in some respects, is worse than a German one. In one point, however, the change is vastly for the better. The opening sentence of Steven-son's article contains an allusion to " that dirty Water of Leith." Thanks to the purification scheme recently

* No. VII., " The Manse."

adopted, the waters are clear again, the foul and mal-odorous sewer has ceased to be, and the angler is happy to find trout in the river once more.

From Colinton we pass on to Slateford, and thence to Edinburgh, either by Craiglockhart or by Gorgie.

PART II

OVER THE HILLS

CHAPTER XII

WALKS ACROSS THE NORTH MASS

Many a glorious walk (long or short) can be taken across the Pentlands from various points north and south of the range. The following chapters describe the main routes, from which the motorist and bicyclist are necessarily and happily excluded, but many of which the equestrian, and all of which the pedestrian, can negotiate. The starting-points mentioned are all on the northern side of the range, and all connected with Edinburgh by rail; the termini on the southern side have also railway connection with the capital; so that one can have less of the hard highway and more of hill and moor in a day's tramp than was possible to the Pentland enthusiasts of a century ago.

I begin with the section of the Pentlands nearest the city—the North Mass, as I have called it—and proceed to indicate the lines and the main features of the walks across it. The three starting-points for these are Colinton, Currie and Balerno, all stations on the Caledonian Railway line which goes up the valley of the Water of Leith.

1. *Colinton to Glencorse or Penicuik* viâ *Bonaly*
(7 *miles or* 7½).

From Edinburgh (Princes Street station) we go to
Colinton by train to save time. Colinton is the first
station * on the little loop-line of railway that ser-
pentines along the steep, rocky and thickly-wooded
banks of the Water of Leith for half a dozen miles. To
those who know that stream—which was until recently believed by the War Office to be navigable for
troopships as far as Edinburgh—only as a variable
trickle of " drumly " beer, flowing under the Dean
Bridge, beloved of suicides, past St Bernard's Well
and the purlieus of Stockbridge, and finally slinking
into the Firth of Forth at the Port of Leith, with all
the fragrance of the Liffey at Dublin—to those who
know the Water of Leith only in these later stages of
its career, the first sight of Colinton Dell comes with
a shock of the most agreeable surprise. The filthy,
doddering old toper, leaning against the wall of his
favourite public-house, is not more unlike the inno-
cent country lad of more than half a century ago
than the Water of Leith, as known to the citizen of
Edinburgh, is unlike the pretty rustic stream that
can be seen from the carriage window, in picturesque
glints and gleams, through holes in heavy curtains of

* Since the above was written the Railway Company have opened a
station at Hailes, between Slateford and Colinton, for the convenience
of the patrons of the new golf-course at Kingsknowe. Golf has now become the chief industry of Edinburgh and district.

foliage that hang over its rocky bed. For dazzling brilliancy and gorgeousness of colouring I know nothing in Scotland to compare with this glen in late autumn, except perhaps the last mile of the Almond from Cramond Brig to the Firth.

Leaving the train at Colinton, and crossing the ravine by a high and narrow old bridge, we scramble up a steep path to the right, which brings us to a road going west. A few hundred yards along this road our path strikes southward and upward toward the mountain-barrier which now faces us. Colinton, an ancient and quaint village, which clings to the steep banks of the Water of Leith, is now being rapidly transformed into a mere suburb of Edinburgh. We are on the hills shortly after leaving the high-road, and immediately after passing Bonaly Tower in its bower of trees, which is associated with the memory of the famous Lord Cockburn, the friend and biographer of Lord Jeffrey. This was his home for more than forty years, and here he died in 1854. " In March 1811," he says, " I married and set up my rural household gods at Bonaly, in the parish of Colinton, close by the northern base of the Pentland Hills; and unless some avenging angel shall expel me, I shall never leave that paradise. I began by an annual lease of a few square yards and a scarcely habitable farmhouse, but, realising the profanations of Auburn, I have destroyed a village and erected a tower, and reached the dignity of a twenty-acred laird. Everything except the two burns, the few old trees, and the mountains, are my own work, and to a great extent the work of my own hands. Human nature is incapable of enjoying more happiness than has been my lot here, where the glories of the prospects, and the luxury of the wild retirement, have been all enhanced by the progress of my improvements, of my children, and of myself. I have been too happy, and often tremble in the anticipation that the cloud must come at last. Warburton says that there was not a bush in his garden on which he had not hung a speculation. There is not a recess in the valleys of the Pentlands, nor an eminence on their summits, that is not familiar to my solitude. One summer I read every word of Tacitus in the sheltered crevice of a rock (called ' My Seat ') about 800 feet above the level of the sea, with the most magnificent of scenes stretched out before me." * It is one of my pardonable ambitions to know the Pentlands as well as Lord Cockburn did—or thought he did—though I own not a yard of them, and can erect no bower of bliss on their heathery slopes.

Having passed Lord Cockburn's retreat, and crossed the Bonaly burn, we begin a steep ascent on a grassy pathway, after a few hundred yards of rough and generally muddy road amongst trees. The green path holds straight up the face of the hill, between barbed-

* *Memorials of his Time*, p. 254. Lord Cockburn has a further allusion to the Pentlands in his account of the foundation of the Edinburgh Academy, which originated with himself and his friend, Leonard Horner : " One day on the top of one of the Pentlands—emblematic of the solidity of our foundation and of the extent of our prospects—we two resolved to set about the establishment of a new school." *Ibid*, p. 415. One would be glad to know which of the Pentland summits is here referred to.

wire fences fringed with large, white, staring notice-
boards, warning against trespass, and hinting dire
penalties by dark allusions to a mysterious " Final
Interdict " of the Court of Session, dated October
1899. I may here remark there is no trespass law in
Scotland, and all such threatened prosecution of tres-
passers is an empty menace to scare the ignorant and
the timid. Mere trespass is not punishable, according
to Scots law. A trespasser may be sued for any damage he has done, but not for simple trespass. A proprietor may apply to the Court of Session for an interdict against you if he finds you trespassing on his
land; that costs him something in the way of trouble
and expense, but costs you nothing. He will probably
get the interdict, and then, if you happen to be caught
again in the same place, you are liable to punishment,
not however for trespass, but for contempt of Court.
The right-of-way up the hill is enclosed, as has been
said, by barbed-wire fences—those brutal evidences
of human selfishness—and it runs along the top of a
deep gully, called the Rocky Ravine, at the foot of
which a little burn bubbles and gurgles, making
merry music as it goes. Here the path is over soft green
turf, and the scenery all around, by tempting us to
frequent pauses to look about us, mitigates the labour
of the climb. On the left, the smooth slopes of Allermuir; to the right the two craggy bluffs of Torduff and
Torphin, the former guarding a reservoir and the
latter crowning a golf-course; in front, Capelaw Hill,
round the west shoulder of which our path will take
us. Near the top of the ascent we pass Bonaly reser-

voir, one of the ten Pentland cisterns * which man's daily need of water has called into existence. The chain of reservoirs round the range would probably look like a necklace of sapphires from an aeroplane. Beyond Bonaly reservoir, the barbed wire and the mysterious warnings about the " Final Interdict " cease to offend the sight, and we find ourselves on a broad, undulating expanse of heathery moorland between Capelaw and Harbour Hill, at an elevation of about 1200 feet, where our intrusion puts up frequent coveys of vociferous grouse, and evokes a shrill protest from the timid curlew. The panorama behind compels us to turn often to contemplate its glories— the hills of Fife, the highlands of Stirling and Perth, the broad valley of the Forth, and the wide fertile plain of the Lothians, not inaptly termed the granary of Scotland. We try not to see the ugly chimneys and the black smoke of the shale districts; we try also not to smell the latter: unsuccessfully, if the wind be in the north west.

Crossing the water-shed, we see opening to the right, that is to the south-west, round the shoulder of Harbour Hill, what is beyond dispute the finest valley in the Pentlands, a deep glen through which flows the Logan burn. It is shut in on its southern side by an imposing rampart of hills, in fact, by the highest mountain mass of the range (the main part of what I call the North Central Mass)—Turnhouse (immediately in

---

* The reservoirs are (besides Bonaly) Torduff and Clubbiedean, close together, Glencorse, Loganlee, Harelaw, Threipmuir, Harper Rig, Crosswood and North Esk. (The last-mentioned is connected with Penicuik.)

front of us), Caernethy, Scald Law, and the two Kips. The north wall of the valley consists principally of the sullen-looking height called the North Black Hill. Towering grandly above them all stands Caernethy, apparently, though not actually, the highest of the chain. It is a curious fact—I do not know if others have observed it, but it has forced itself on my notice again and again—that from every point of view Caernethy looks higher than Scald Law, though the latter is really the higher of the two. Even when one is looking at Caernethy across Scald Law, from the top of the West Kip, Caernethy seems to be the higher; and I am sure that anyone, ignorant of the actual measurements, looking at the Pentlands from the north, or the south, or indeed any point of view, would unhesitatingly declare that Caernethy was the highest of them all. This optical illusion is probably due to the bolder outline of Caernethy, which is gracefully conical, while Scald Law is rounder on the shoulders and flat at the top. " I think," wrote Sir Walter Scott in his *Journal*, " I never saw anything more beautiful than the ridge of Caernethy against a clear, frosty sky, with its peaks and varied slopes. The hills glowed like purple amethyst, the sky glowed topaz and vermilion colours. I never saw a finer screen than Pentland, considering that it is neither rocky nor highly elevated." * Scott's view-point, however, was several miles to the eastward of our present position, if he is merely recording the impression of an evening drive from Lasswade to Edinburgh, in which con-

* *Journal*, Nov. 11, 1827.

Drummond Young & Watson]

[Edinburgh

LOGANLEE VALLEY

[To face page 104

nection the above passage was written. Scott, however, knew Caernethy well from a nearer point of
view, namely Woodhouselee and Castlelaw.

Straight below us in the valley lies the Glencorse
reservoir, unpoetically called the Compensation Pond,
which is fed by the Logan burn and a few small
streams. Between Castlelaw Hill, which is now on
our left, and Turnhouse Hill across the valley, the eye
sweeps an extensive champaign of field and wood,
stretching away to the south-eastern horizon, which
is bounded by the undulating outline of the Muirfoot
Hills. The chimneys of the factories and coal-pits in
and near Penicuik can be seen belching forth their
black smoke above the trees in the distance. A steep
descent brings us to a carriage-road leading from
Loganlee to the high-road, where we turn to the left
along the north bank of the reservoir. Near the point
where the Kirk burn flows into the reservoir there
lie, under the waters, the very fragmentary remains
of the chapel called St Catharine-in-the-Hopes.* As
the barrage of the Nile has submerged the historic
island of Philæ, so the dam here has swallowed up
this ancient sanctuary. The story goes that King
Robert the Bruce and William St Clair, the ancestor
of the earls of Rosslyn, were out together on a hunting expedition on the north side of the Pentlands.

* *i.e.* St Catharine among the valleys. This name seems to give some
confirmation to one of the suggested derivations of the name Carlops.
See p. 42. It is not clear whether the virgin and martyr of Alexandria, or
the lady of Sienna, is commemorated by this chapel. The former is certainly connected by ecclesiastical legend with the neighbourhood of Liberton : the Balm Well of St Catharine's.

They did strange things in those days when the sporting instinct was uppermost. St Clair wagered his head against a part of the royal lands that his two hounds "Help" and "Hauld," would bring down a white deer they had started before it could cross the Logan Water. The wager was accepted by the king, and won by St Clair, who thereupon built a chapel to St Catharine to mark the spot for all time, not dreaming, alas, of the vandalism of future Water Trusts! It might be interesting to know what good King Robert would have done if the deer had escaped St Clair's hounds.* The legend may or may not have some foundation in fact, but it is certain that this was from early times an ecclesiastical neighbourhood. Glencorse is a corruption of Glen Cross, and Chalmers in his *Caledonia* says the name was derived " from a remarkable cross which had once been erected in the Vale of Glencross by pious hands and which also gave the name to Crosshouses."† With the irritating vagueness characteristic of writers of his time, Chalmers omits to indicate the spot where this cross was erected, does not mention the why and wherefore of its erection, and gives no information to throw light on many questions that modern interest and curiosity would put to him on the subject.

We now follow the carriage-way to the high-road,

---

* The end of the legend is at Glencorse reservoir ; its beginning is at Threipmuir. See p. 115.

St Clair's tomb is in Roslin Chapel. The above legend is alluded to in the lines—

> " Help and Hauld, on ye may,
> Or Rosslyn will lose his head this day ! "

† See p. 25.

Drummond Young & Watson] ST CATHARINE'S CHAPEL, GLENCORSE

[Edinburgh.

[To face page 106.

which we enter at Flotterstane Brig,* and, turning to the left, we keep the road for nearly half a mile till we reach the farm of Crosshouse, whence a beautifully-wooded winding by-road on the right leads to Glencorse. (The route from the reservoir to this point may be slightly varied by taking the path up the hillside to Castlelaw farm, and thence down to Crosshouse.) The first thing we note on the way to Glencorse village is a low structure like a Greek temple on the green haugh which slopes down to the water-side. This covers the cistern of the famous Crawley Spring, which from 1819 has supplied Edinburgh with its waters. About half a mile further on, standing above the road on the left, is old Glencorse parish church, well worth a visit. This is generally accepted as the church which figures in Robert Louis Stevenson's *Weir of Hermiston*. It is a picturesque heap of ivy-clad ruins, crowned by a black wooden belfry suggestive of bats, owls and jackdaws. The little transept, which is apparently the most modern part, bears the date 1699. Gravestones of considerable antiquity stand or lie about the churchyard, but for the most part their inscriptions have been rendered illegible by time, moss and lichen. Another half-mile brings us past the new parish church, with its quaint red-tiled tower standing high above the surrounding trees, to the Fishers' Tryst inn, whence the high-road to the right leads past the Glencorse barracks to the railway station.

Another delightful and invigorating walk from Bonaly to Glencorse may be indicated in a few words.

* See p. 25.

It is the same as that described above, as far as the watershed,* whence we keep round the shoulder of Capelaw Hill towards the ruins of Capelaw farm, which are visible on the bleak hillside. There is a scarcely distinguishable path to this farm (a few yards short of the first post of the Scottish Rights-of-Way Society) leading downwards into the hollow, across the burn, and up the slope on the opposite side. The ruined farm looks very desolate indeed, with its roofless gables, its grass-grown kailyaird, a few scraggy trees, and a forlorn dry-stane dyke enclosing an irregular polygon of what was once a field, at the foot of which the lonely Kirk burn hurries towards the reservoir below. Our path leads past this ruined " toun," and makes for the pass between Capelaw and Allermuir, the head of which is a gate in the march-dyke. From this a climb of less than 400 feet, taking a bee-line, will bring us to the top of Allermuir. That not being in contemplation at present, walk a few yards to the north of the gate, when you will see through a cleft in the hills the little village of Colinton far below in its nest of trees. When the day is clear and the sun shining on it, this view, framed as it is by the near hill slopes, is one of the prettiest imaginable. From the gate we hold southwards, crossing the rounded top of Fala Knowe † (1434 ft.) and keeping along the eastern shoulder of Castlelaw Hill. Weather and light being favourable, I know no better coign of

* See p. 103.

† This must be distinguished from another and smaller Fala Knowe to the south of Caernethy.

vantage than Fala Knowe for seeing, and getting a good general impression of, the lie and character of the North and North Central masses of the Pentlands. The view on both sides of our path is extensive and impressive. The long dark vista of the Logan valley has no rival in the whole range for scenic beauty. The hills that form the valley are to be seen in all their stately grandeur, enclosing the steel-blue waters of Loganlee, while the horizon to the west is shut in by the dark and distant outline of the East Cairn Hill. On the other hand, to the east, Caerketton presents a fissured or segmented appearance which is not visible from the plains below. We now descend Castlelaw Hill to the farm that takes its name from its site, having in front of us a magnificent prospect of the wide plains watered by the two Esks. A few hundred yards above the farm traces of an old Pictish fort are to be seen. Castlelaw Farm is associated with the memory of John Wood, " the King of the Pentlands," who was for nearly fifty years shepherd here, a well-known character in the district, whose name deserves to be handed down to posterity along with that of John Todd immortalised by Robert Louis Stevenson.* He was one of those rugged, forceful, somewhat eccentric personalities that make a deep and lasting impression on the minds and affections of their fellows. Wood died in 1901, having nearly completed his ninety-sixth year. There is a good road from the farm to Crosshouse, whence we go to Glencorse by the route already described.†

* *Memories and Portraits*, No. VI.   † See p. 107.

Those who desire to go to Penicuik, instead of to Glencorse, leave the carriage-way half-way between the reservoir and Flotterstane Brig, taking a path to the right which crosses the burn by a foot-bridge, and goes straight to the House of Muir.* (Of course they can get to the same spot by keeping the road to Flotterstane, and turning up the hill to the right in the high-road.) Leaving the high-road a few hundred yards above the House of Muir, at the house called Martyrs' Cross,† a by-road goes southward between the richly-wooded policies of Bellwood and Mauricewood. Mauricewood is a tragic name deeply graven in the memory of Scottish miners and of the dwellers in this neighbourhood, for the pit—situated to the right of the roadway about a mile beyond Martyrs' Cross—was the scene of one of the most disastrous colliery explosions in the annals of our country (1889). There is nothing in the aspect of the pit to-day, which is as busy as ever,‡ to remind the casual passer-by of that awful calamity, but the memory of it haunts him, and he wonders, as he takes his onward way, how Nature can smile so placidly, and men go about their work so calmly, on a spot of such dreadful associations. The busy little town of Penicuik is reached after another mile-and-a-half's tramp, and here one has the choice of railway or motor-omnibus to convey him to Edinburgh.

The walk just described is one of the easiest of the trans-Pentland expeditions from Edinburgh, conse-

* The distance by this route is, roughly, 7 miles.
† See p. 26.   ‡ The pit was closed in 1909.

quently it is better known than others which take pedestrians further afield.

2. *Currie to Glencorse or Penicuik (6¾ miles or 7¼).*

The greater part of this route has been already dealt with: all that has to be noted in this section is the line of walk from Currie to the Glencorse reservoir. Leaving the train at Currie station we cross Currie Brig,* and take the road past the parish church —the Kirk Loan—keeping straight on till we reach a gate, by which is a post of the Scottish Rights-of-Way Society, whence there is visible another of the Society's posts a quarter of a mile distant. We make for that, passing the Malleny shooting-range on the left, and reach the old drove road that connected the Balerno district with the House of Muir market.† There are not a few such roads across the Pentlands, and of these Stevenson says: "The drove roads lay apart from habitation; the drovers met in the wilderness as to-day the deep-sea fishers meet off the banks in the solitude of the Atlantic, and in the one as in the other case rough habits and fist-law were the rule. Crimes were committed, sheep filched, and drovers robbed and beaten; most of which offences had a moorland burial and were never heard of in the courts of justice." ‡ A series of posts, indicating our way to the left, though their guidance is scarcely necessary here, lead us through the Maiden's Cleugh, between Harbour Hill and Bell's Hill, on the track of

* See p. 95.　　† See p. 26.　　‡ *Memories and Portraits*, No. VI.

Dalzell's dragoons,* to a post marking the junction of our present path with that from Bonaly, just above the Glencorse reservoir. In winter, when there are great patches of snow on the sombre hills of the North Central Mass, when the boggy bits of the road are frozen solid, and the path rings like an anvil under one's iron-shod heels, a more delightful walk than that through the Maiden's Cleugh could scarcely be conceived.

The adventurous may cross the drove road, and hold straight on through Dens Cleugh, going round the south-western shoulder of Bell's Hill, and coming down on the reservoir at the back of Kirkton. This is not a right-of-way; indeed, there is a notice pointedly declaring that there is " No road this way," but the proprietor will, I trust, forgive me when I confess that I have occasionally made a road for myself that way, and enjoyed it greatly. Only in winter, however, when there was no fear of disturbing game, interrupting shooters, or doing any kind of damage.

3. *Balerno to Glencorse or Penicuik* viâ *Harelaw* (8 *miles or* 8¼).

The greater part of this route has already been described in the previous sections. We take the road that passes through Balerno village, and, when it divides, keep to the left. The road now skirts the right bank of the Bavelaw burn. Half a mile beyond the Malleny mills we turn to the left, and at Harelaw to

* See pp. 29, 95.

the right again. After a short distance we get upon
the drove road mentioned above, and follow the line
of the Rights-of-Way Society's posts to the Maiden's
Cleugh. To the south of our path lies the Harelaw
reservoir, added to the Edinburgh water system in
1843.

H

CHAPTER XIII

WALKS ACROSS THE NORTH CENTRAL MASS

1. *Balerno to Penicuik* vià *Bavelaw, Loganlee and the Old Kirk Road* (9 *miles*).

BALERNO village offers little interest to the passer-by. It stands chiefly on two sides of a steep street, and is mainly remarkable for not having anything you may happen to want. Having forgotten to take a handkerchief with me one morning, I visited all the shops in search of that useful article, but found it not. One may draw several inferences from that fact, most of them probably wrong. South of the village, where the road forks, we keep to the right, a winding, undulating, and in places prettily-wooded road taking us past Marchbank and the deserted hamlet of Redford to Threipmuir. Between Marchbank and Threipmuir an extensive panorama of the Pentlands comes in sight. To the left is the North Black Hill, next to which is Hare Hill, with the peak of Caernethy appearing between them. Westward of Hare Hill are to be seen, in order, the West Kip, the comb of the Spittal Hill, Cock Rig, Wether Law and the two Cairn Hills. Threipmuir is said to have got its name from the legend of

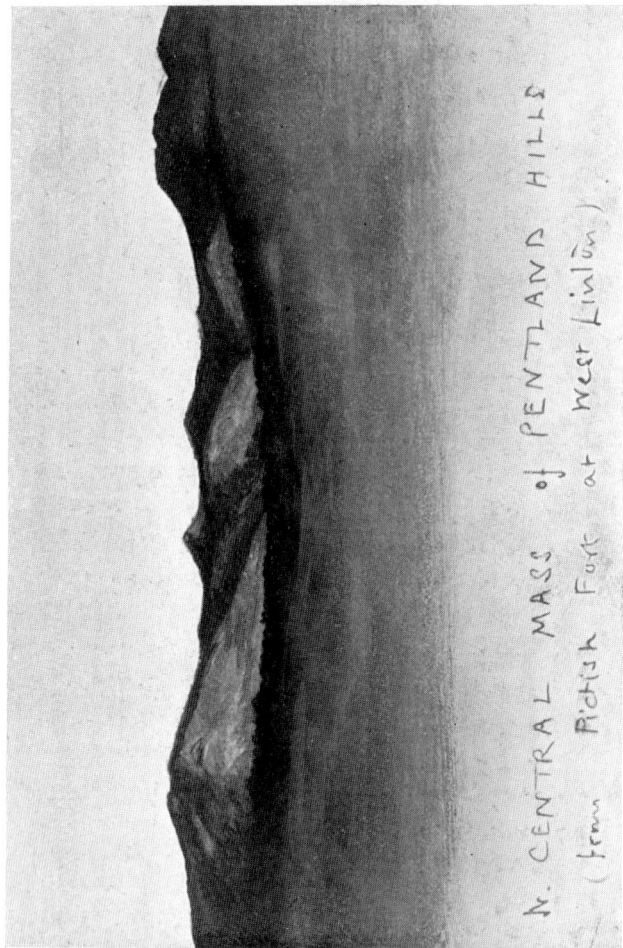

N. CENTRAL MASS of PENTLAND HILLS
(from Pictish Fort at West Linton).

Drummond Young & Watson]

(From a Water-Colour Sketch by the Author)

[Edinburgh

[To face page 114

Robert the Bruce and Sir William St Clair narrated in the last chapter.* Somewhere in this neighbourhood the hunters started the "white faunch deer," which made for Loganlee. Sir William "threipit" his hounds "Help" and "Hauld" after their fleet quarry, and hence the name, according to tradition. There is a large reservoir here made by damming the waters of the Bavelaw and Denscleugh burns, together with some other smaller streams. It was constructed in 1843. We cross this by a low bridge, on which one is tempted to stand for some time watching the numerous wildfowl on the waters, and enjoying the beauties of the prospect all around. We then go up a steep, straight, well-shaded avenue towards Bavelaw Castle. At the top of the ascent the road divides: we take the path to the left, and skirting the castle enclosure climb a stile, and find ourselves on a fine stretch of breezy moorland. The ancient keep, which holds our eyes for a few moments as we pass, is said to have been a hunting-seat of the Scottish kings. In the days of yore a vast royal hunting domain extended westwards from Edinburgh, and seems to have embraced most of the lands from the Pentlands to the Firth of Forth.†

Guided by the Rights-of-Way Society posts, though the pathway is well marked, we cross the moor towards Hare Hill, round the east shoulder of which we enter the Green Cleugh, a narrow winding valley whose quiet beauty lends a charm to our walk. At first its name is justified by the colour of the soft green turf

* See p. 105.   † See Appendix A.

and the verdure all around. In spring the grouse seem to make this spot a kind of " Lovers' Loan," for the cock-birds are to be seen courting the other sex with the most extraordinary antics and no little noise. Later on the beauty of the valley becomes sterner and wilder; it loses its greenness to a great extent, and the Black Hill descends abruptly upon us in what looks like cataracts of road-metal.

Ere we emerge from the valley we see, on the right, a slender waterfall zigzagging between two rounded crags, and ending in a deep, crystal pool. This has long been known as " Habbie's Howe," and by the irreverent it is now called " the false Habbie's Howe." The dispute between the advocates of this spot and those of Newhall * as the scene of Allan Ramsay's *Gentle Shepherd* threatened at one time to assume the proportions and develop the acrimony of the controversy as to the innocence of Mary Queen of Scots. John Hill Burton acutely remarked with regard to the latter that the innocence of Mary was with many a creed rather than an opinion; and one might safely say the same of those who would localise Allan Ramsay's pastoral drama here. There are no trees; there is nothing to suggest the rich verdure of the poem; there is no " flowrie howm "; the district is rather wild and bare. But the waterfall makes a pleasant *terminus ad quem* for picnic parties, and is largely taken advantage of by these. If any take with them a copy of *The Gentle Shepherd*, in the belief that they are going to " Habbie's Howe," they will wonder

* See p. 37.

what enchanter has stripped the landscape of the special features therein described.

Miss Warrender has complicated the controversy by putting in a plea for a third locality. " I have been told," she writes, " by Mr Stillie, who has good reasons for knowing the truth of the matter, that Allan Ramsay laid the scenery of *The Gentle Shepherd* round the Hunter's Tryst,* and that

> " A flowrie howm between twa verdant braes,
>   Where lasses use to wash and spread their claes;
>   A trottin' burnie wimplin' thro' the ground,
>   Its channel pebbles shining smooth and round,"

lies down in the hollow at the bottom of the hill by the Braid burn. Mr Trotter of the Bush was very anxious to establish the fact that Habbie's Howe was up the Logan Water in Glencorse, and Mr Brown of Newhall claimed the site for his property further west along the Pentlands, and wrote a book to prove that he was right. In consequence it is the generally-received opinion that the spot now called Habbie's Howe, or Newhall, was the one intended by Allan Ramsay; but, according to the tradition received by my informant from Allan Ramsay's friends and relations, both were wrong." †

I am afraid that, despite Mr Stillie's authority, public faith in the genuineness of the Newhall site will not be shaken. It should be remembered that Ramsay was well acquainted with Newhall, being often an honoured guest of the then proprietor, Mr John

* See p. 13.
† *Walks near Edinburgh.*   Second edition (1895), p. 33, *note.*

Forbes, and it should also be remembered that poets, like artists, are given to " mixing " their scenery.

From the waterfall we descry a post on the hillside to the south-east. Making our way to which we cross a burn with steep banks at a place called " the Lover's Loup "—Allan Ramsay again—and see on our left the noble stretch of the Logan valley * with a bonnie loch in the foreground. This sheet of water does not in the least look like a reservoir at this point, yet it is one. A good road runs from the head of it to Flotter-stane Brig. It skirts the base of the North Black Hill on its way to the Glencorse reservoir, and is remark-able for the number of ruins upon it—Loganlee, at the head of the loch, the Howlet's House about half-way down, and Logan Tower half-way between the two reservoirs. Our route is now the old Kirk Road, which goes steeply up the side of Scald Law, and, as we mount it, hot and breathless, gives us new ideas about the sturdy piety and physical endurance of our ancestors who weekly took this path to church. It suggests also invidious comparisons with their de-generate descendants in both respects. Reaching the summit of the pass (1456 feet—we have risen 500 feet in half a mile), let us turn and look round. On the right, Caernethy's fine cone stands grandly above us. To the left, across the broad shoulder of Scald Law, appears the East Kip. In front are the crags above the alleged " Habbie's Howe," with Hare Hill in the background, and the steep dark sides of the Black Hill, looking for all the world like a dirty patched

* See pp. 103 *et seq.*

gipsy tent. Below, the dark blue waters of Loganlee. From this point the top of Scald Law or of Caernethy —or both if one be very energetic—can be easily attained, and the view from either is, on a clear day, a rich reward for all the labour expended in the ascent. The Pentlands are so placed that from no other hills in Scotland of the same height can a view at once so extensive and so varied be obtained.

Resuming our walk we begin a break-neck descent down the deep gully between Caernethy and Scald Law, keeping close to the Grain burn, which seems to get lost in a bog rather more than half-way down. It reappears again, however, before we reach the high-road, but now bears the name of Loam burn. We turn to the left by the high-road, and then to the right at Coates farm, whence a delightful woodland path winding along the left bank of the Loam burn brings us into Penicuik. In summer this walk through the woods is a rare delight, and at all seasons the bed of the burn presents features interesting to the geologist.

2. Balerno to Penicuik viâ Bavelaw, Kitchen Moss and the West Kip (9¾ miles).

The route in this walk is the same as the foregoing so far as the top of the avenue near Bavelaw Castle, where the road divides. We now turn to the right for a few yards, and then to the left again, at a gate where a post indicates that our path lies that way.

We are now out on the moors, proceeding southwards by a gentle ascent, casting many an admiring look behind at the gradually-expanding panorama of eastern and central Scotland. We descend a little after surmounting one or two ridges, and cross the Logan burn by an ancient and rather tumble-down bridge, which looks as if it might have been built by the Romans and left to the assiduous neglect of the county authorities ever since. The stream is called the Logan burn in maps; it was formerly the Kitchen burn, and the boggy waste of moorland it traverses is still known as the Kitchen Moss. At the old bridge, where we are at present standing, it is merely a little deep-sunk beck; but on its way to the plains it has a very picturesque and romantic course.* From the bridge we follow the path up the right shoulder of the West Kip, which hill has the sharpest outline of all the Pentlands. It is a very slightly truncated cone, with a little nick on the western side. Its summit (1806 feet above sea-level) is an extremely narrow, rocky plat-form a few yards long—a sort of knife-edge—and the view obtainable on a clear day is magnificent. At least twelve counties can be descried, from Perth in the north to Selkirk and Berwick in the south and east. Perhaps more. The difficulty is to get a perfectly clear day. The facts above indicated represent the observa-tions of many days; never yet have I seen the full circle of the horizon clear and distinct; there is always cloud, mist or haze about somewhere, and to the north-west the chimneys of the oil-country and of the

* This is the water that ultimately joins the North Esk near Auchen-dinny, changing its name several times *en route*. From its source to Lo-ganlee it is the Kitchen burn; from Loganlee reservoir to Glencorse reservoir it is the Logan Water; thereafter it is known as the Glencorse burn.

THE TWO KIPS
(*From Camp Hill*)

[To face page 120

iron-works about Falkirk not only pollute the atmosphere in their immediate neighbourhood, but obscure the view in that direction. Which is trying to those who are not shareholders in either oil or iron companies.

The path we are in, however, takes us through a pass 300 feet below the top of West Kip—between that peak and Gap Law—whence we have a choice of two routes downward; one by the west side of the gully before us, leading across Braid Law to Nine-Mile-Burn,* the other taking the east side—our present route—skirting the dark and heavy shoulder of the South Black Hill, and joining the Biggar road just beyond the tiny ruins of Saltersyke. Thence, turning to the left along the high-road, and passing through the hamlet of Silverburn,† we reach Coates farm, whence down through the woods by the Loam burn to Penicuik.

3. *Balerno to Nine-Mile-Burn and Carlops* vià *the West Kip* (7 *miles and* 8½).

The two previous sections describe the walk as far as the pass between the West Kip and Gap Law. From that point the right-of-way, marked by posts, holds down the hillside to the west of the gully, skirts a large wood, crosses Braid Law and the side of Pillar Knowe behind Walstone farm, crosses the moor, and joins the old Biggar high-road a few hundred yards above Nine-Mile-Burn inn.

It is a more interesting walk, however, to leave the right-of-way at the summit of the pass and take the

* See p. 36.　　　　　† See p. 33.

path—it is not very distinct in places—that strikes due south across the top of Gap Law, and by it make for the Spittal farm. This is the old Monks' road,* on the left side of which, on the Monks' Rig, the southern shoulder of Gap Law, there stands a shallow stone trough, called the Font Stane, the exact purpose of which has been forgotten. It formed part of some larger structure, for it is described as a " stone with a trough in its middle, two excavations on its side as if for a person's knees, and a socket at its end for a cross." In 1808, when this description was written—in an elaborate edition of *The Gentle Shepherd*—the head of the cross was said to be still lying at the foot of the Monks' Rig. The stone scarcely corresponds to the description now; time and weather have worn it thin and shallow.

Beyond the Font Stane there is a steep declivity to the Monks' burn. To the north, the graceful, rounded cone of the Green Law fills the horizon; it is part of the long verdant ridge of turf which is now generally called the Spittal Hill. From the Monks' burn we ascend again, cross Dod † Hill, which is crowned with

* " An old deserted way-worn track, called the Monks' Road, pointing along it (the Monks' Rig) to Queensferry and Edinburgh, with its fount-stone on its brow, is conspicuously in view. It commands all the south country ; and the ornamented top of its cross, formerly erected on the edge of the fount-stone, is still lying at the foot of the Rig."—Brown's *Notes on Pennicuik.* The cross has now wholly disappeared.

† Evidently the Scandinavian *Toddi*, a foot-hill or slight elevation near a mountain mass. There is another small hill to the north of this, also a spur of the Spittal Hill, which is locally called the Dod Knowe, but is not marked so on the Ordnance Survey map. An old map of the district, dated 1770, calls the latter the Upper, and the former the Nether, Dod Rig.

an old sheepfold, a maze of drystane dykes, and in the hollow behind come upon a little burn, on the opposite bank of which stands the Spittal farm. There is history in that name, but tradition has largely forgotten the details. The name Spittal is fairly common in Scotland, and usually marks the site either of a wayside refuge for pilgrims and other travellers, or of a lazar-house, erected and maintained by some monkish fraternity. The place-names of a very large district in this neighbourhood preserve—I cannot say the memory but—the traces of the monks of Newhall, who belonged to the Cistercian order. Their monastery, the centre of their beneficent operations, seems to have been on the banks of the North Esk, near the present mansion of Newhall, and though it is not safe to infer numbers from the quality and quantity of the work done, yet it may be regarded as probable that the establishment was by no means a small one. That they had a *hospitium* near the Spittal farm is beyond doubt. The Ordnance Survey map indicates the site of it on a narrow strip of green sward just across the burn from the farm. Notwithstanding this, I have reasons for thinking that the real site is on the top of Dod Hill, where the sheep-fold is—one of the strongest reasons being the fact that, if the *hospitium* stood where it is placed by local tradition, it would have been invisible to travellers until they were within a few hundred yards of it. Part of the monkish settlement may have been on that strip—perhaps the main part—but I cannot believe that the summit of the Dod Hill, which can be seen afar from all directions, was not marked by a building of some kind, and personal examination of the spot on several occasions has confirmed me in this belief. The farm-house of Spittal is modern, but the cart-shed occupies the site, and embodies some of the materials of the old mansion house of Spittal. Here dwelt James Oswald, accidentally shot near Slipperfield Loch by one of his keepers, the man whose dinner-table was made his tombstone.* On a knoll to the south of the farmhouse lie the ruins of Upper Friartown † (locally pronounced Freretown), while near the point where the cart-road from the Spittal farm joins the old Edinburgh and Biggar highroad stood Nether Friartown, almost opposite what used to be the entrance to Newhall from the turnpike, before the present highway was in existence. Adjoining Nether Friartown, to the east, is a patch of land that still bears the name of St Robert's Croft. St Robert was a Benedictine monk who founded the congregation of Cistercians towards the end of the eleventh century (1098). The association of his name, therefore, with this district is appropriate. The building on the site of the farm used to be called the Fore Spittal to distinguish it from the Back Spittal,‡ the ruins of which lie on the left bank of the North Esk river on the other side of the hill. This latter may have been—and from its isolated position I think it probably was—a lazar-house connected with the

* See p. 68.

† John Todd, "the roaring shepherd" of Swanston, immortalised by R. L. Stevenson, was born, and spent the early part of his married life, here.

‡ See p. 132.

monastery. Leprosy was rife in Scotland until the fourteenth century, from which time it gradually died out. It is not unlikely that these spittals were used not only for lepers but also for patients suffering from any kind of " smittal " disease, notably small-pox. The presence in this wide district of so many out-houses, so to speak, of the Newhall establishment—the Upper and Nether Friartowns, the Fore and Back Spittals, and some other buildings, traces of which are to be seen near Habbie's Howe—seems to indicate that these friars exercised both an extensive and a varied hospitality, religious, medical and eleemosynary.* Leaving the Spittal farm we soon reach the old Biggar road, on which we may either turn to the left and rest for a while at Nine-Mile-Burn inn † (where Allan Ramsay's influence is again in evidence on a poetical sign-board), or to the right, and go to Carlops, where the picturesque old highway, skirting the base of Patie's Hill, reaches the modern turnpike a few yards short of the village.

4. *Balerno to Nine-Mile-Burn* viâ *the Green Law and the Spittal Hill.*

This is a very delightful walk. The route is the

* " Besides being a receptacle for the sick and superannuated, the 'Spitals were probably each a *hospitium* or inn, and with the rood, and its fonts and crosses, which also served as landmarks, an accommodation for travellers passing from one monastery to another, the Back 'Spital such as went by the north side of the hill. In confirmation of this the weary and benighted traveller is still regarded as having a right, from use and wont, to shelter and protection at the Fore 'Spital, and one of the out-houses with some straw is generally allotted for that purpose."— Brown's *Notes on Pennicuik.*

† See p. 36.

same as that described on p. 120, as far as the bridge over the Kitchen burn, from which point take a bee-line (as nearly as the bog will permit) to the top of the Green Law, which stands due south from the bridge. Beyond the intervening marsh there is a gentle ascent over soft turf to the summit, whose verdure accounts for its name. There is no right-of-way here, and no path except a network of sheep-trails, but the walking is easy and the view is unspeakably fine on a clear day. To the north-east nearly the whole of the North, and North Central masses can be seen; to the south-west stretches the broad green ridge of the Spittal Hill, along which our route now takes us. We have, as we proceed, an uninterrupted view of the country north and south of the Pentland range. Our path is up and down here and there, but in the main it is tolerably level. We pass the Greystane Head, the highest point of the Spittal Hill, shortly after which the North Esk reservoir comes into sight far below on the right. A few hundred yards further on, and apparently a little to the right of the axis of the ridge, there is what is described on the Ordnance Survey map as a " petrifying well," for which many in the neighbourhood, not to mention myself, have searched in vain. A little further on we reach a march-dyke, where we strike the path between the reservoir and Nine-Mile-Burn described on p. 132.

Note.—Redford (p. 114) is destined to suffer an invasion which all patriotic Scots welcome. It is to be the site of a new barracks for cavalry and infantry.

CHAPTER XIV

WALKS ACROSS THE SOUTH CENTRAL MASS

ACROSS the South Central Mass there is only one right-of-way, but, as this can be approached from many different points, the walk can be agreeably varied. From all points it is a very pleasant and by no means heavy walk.

1. *Balerno to Carlops* viâ *the Bore Stane* (9½ *miles*).

Two and a half miles along the Lanark road westwards from Balerno station, some distance beyond the Boll of Bear farm, and facing a belt of woodland, a side-road strikes southward past Haugh Head farm, and, crossing the Water of Leith, keeps straight for the hills by a gentle ascent on a tolerable road, which ends not far from the farm of Listonshiels—the house we see in front of us, slightly to the right, in a bower of trees. Thereafter we find ourselves on the heathery hillside, crossing a wide expanse of moorland to the west of the Kitchen Moss,* guided by posts of the Rights-of-Way Society. At this point—for the path makes directly for what is very nearly the middle of the range—almost the whole northern sweep of the Pentlands is in view, from Allermuir to West Cairn

* See p. 126.

Hill. Compared with the bolder and more rugged scenery of the Highlands it cannot be called an imposing view—the *coup d'œil* is much more striking from the other side of the hills—still, to those who have often crossed their boggy outworks, scaled their heathery *glacis*, and devoured sandwiches on their ramparts, even the comparatively tame aspect of their northern slopes has a charm of its own.

We soon reach the banks of the Bavelaw burn, the course of which our path hugs till we pass its source. The heights immediately in front of us are Cock Rig, to the left, and the gloomy East Cairn Hill to the right, with a ridge between them, up the slopes of which we have now to scramble. The latter is the bleakest and most sombre-looking in the range. It is a heavy, snail-shaped, rocky—or rather stony—hill, of sullen and uninviting appearance. One very rarely sees it clear of mist. Following the right bank of the Bavelaw burn, and crossing a very deep syke * by what might be mistaken for a natural bridge, the path, after a few hundred yards more of rather steep ascent, reaches the summit of the pass at an elevation of 1250 feet. Looking backward, we see the land rapidly sinking towards the green plain of the Lothians, while at the edge of a lonely little copse, which seems surprised to find itself there, amid such a waste of moorland, we espy a pile of rocks—one had better, in strict accuracy, say an outcrop of rocks—which one might easily pass by

* A syke is a deep channel, gully or *nullah*, at the foot of which a burn runs. The sykes in the Pentlands often present in miniature the appearance of the cañons of Colorado.

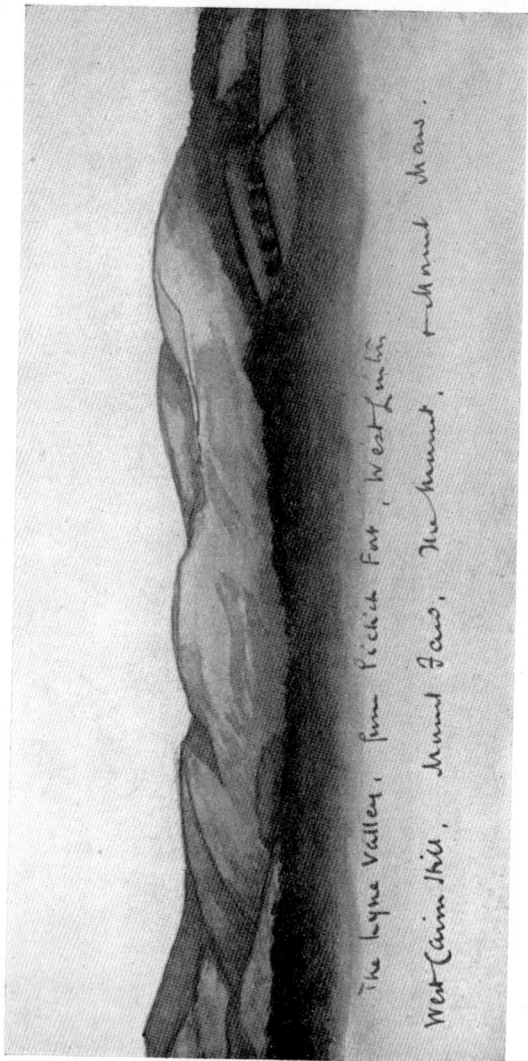

The Lyne Valley, from Pickie Fort, West Linton, West Cairn Hill, Mount Maw, the Mount, about Shaw.

Drummond Young & Watson]

(From a Water-Colour Sketch by the Author)

without particular notice, and which, though plural in number, rejoices, nobody knows why, in the singular name of the Bore Stane. Elsewhere in Scotland a bore-stane is a stone on which the royal standard was unfurled on some historic occasion. There is one in Edinburgh, let into the wall near Morningside parish church, the stone on which the standard of James IV. was set at the great muster on the Boroughmuir, previous to his fatal march to Flodden field. There is another, of happier augury for Scotland, near the field of Bannockburn, where Bruce's banner flew. But there is no record of any muster in this wild solitude. It is possible that the tramp of Roman legions startled the curlew, as these adventurers went up to look over the Pentland screen into the valley of the Forth; but we do not know that they were actually here, and we do not associate bore-stanes with them. Further, the rocks so-called here are not in the least like the other bore-stanes we know. Some would write the name " Boar Stane," but even so its purport is still a mystery. It is, however, a county landmark, for it is the point of one of the wedges that Peeblesshire * drives

* I once was an interested and amused listener to a hot discussion between two shepherds as to whether Mendick, near West Linton, was of the Pentlands or no. The one maintained that the geography books described the Pentlands as a range in Midlothian ; Mendick, being in Peeblesshire, could not therefore be part of them. The other contended that it belonged to the general mountain-mass of the district, which existed before county boundaries were drawn and geography books compiled.   They finally referred the matter to me as arbiter, and I decided for the latter, pointing out at the same time that the hills north of Dunsyre were also of the Pentlands, though their roots were struck in Lanarkshire. I doubt whether the shepherd of the geography books was convinced : great faith has the rustic mind in a " prynt buik."

I

northward into the Pentland range. It is the most
northerly of these. Close by it a little trickle flowing
southward shows that we have crossed the watershed; and this streamlet, for six miles of its course, is
the boundary between Midlothian and Peeblesshire,
for it is the North Esk, down the left bank of which
our path now takes us. The scenery assumes the
austere wildness that one naturally associates with
the remote Highlands. We thread the pass between
the dark East Cairn Hill and Cock Rig, having
Wether Law and The Mount in front. At the top of the
sombre ravine to the right, down which curves the
Henshaw burn, one Thomson, an Edinburgh lawyer,
built himself a house a hundred and sixty years ago.
Local critics called it unsympathetically " The Folly."
What his object was in seeking a lodge in this vast
wilderness does not appear; but the gloomy grandeur
of its surroundings would strongly appeal to men of a
solitary and meditative temperament. Thomson found
no successor to his hermitage, and the house has disappeared. As our path winds down the glen, the
scenery softens in aspect, the turf is green and springy
under our feet, and when we round the southern
shoulder of Cock Rig, the pretty little shield-shaped
North Esk reservoir suddenly comes in sight. This is
a mountain tarn that has been widened and deepened
by a huge dam, whose smooth green *glacis* blends
naturally with the colour of the surrounding landscape. It is a compensation pond to keep the North
Esk supplied with sufficient water to meet the de-
mands made on it by the paper-makers of Penicuik.

Here dwell some splendid trout, compulsory emigrants from the far-famed Loch Leven, which, while they excite the angler's hopes, generally succeed in putting a fine edge on his disappointment. They show themselves freely on a favourable day, but are shy of coming to the point. That is no doubt better for them, but it exasperates the sportsman. Happy is he who can take the rubs of fortune with equanimity! The fishing here is private, but the proprietors are generous with permission to respectable applicants. The reservoir lies in a deep cup, shut in on all sides except the south, by The Mount, Wether Law, Cock Rig and the Spittal Hill; the consequence of this situation is that before the angler can have a satisfactory " curl " on the water, the wind must be blowing half a gale. Even when the wind is high, large stretches of the water remain calm, so closely do the steep hillsides come to the water's edge. At the south end of the reservoir stands the keeper's cottage, and Mr William Todd, who occupies it with his family, will forgive me for saying that he is a worthy with whom all Pentland enthusiasts delight to have a " crack," for he is one who possesses a great stock of local information, a fund of pawky anecdote, and a poetical gift of no mean order. He is a son of John Todd whom Stevenson has made famous, and was born at Upper Friartown.* He has collected in his house a number of objects of interest, and specially interesting are his photographs of a great antiquarian " find " recently made in the neighbourhood. Towards the north shore

* See p. 124, *note*.

of the reservoir there is a small island crowned by a few trees. On this island some old coffins were dug up, which are supposed to have been laid there by the monks of the Spittal * many centuries ago. In the valley below the reservoir, on the left bank of the river, at the foot of the southern slope of the Spittal Hill, there may be seen traces of a small building erected by the monks of Newhall—possibly as a hospital for some special disease.† From the keeper's cottage a path goes eastward over the ridge between the Spittal Hill and Patie's Hill, and goes down past the Spittal farm ‡ to the old road between Nine-Mile-Burn and Carlops. The Spittal Hill, whose long eastern side looks very uninteresting as seen from the Biggar road, appears as a sharp ridge when viewed from the south-west.

Our path, however, takes us southward, high above the river, till the farm of Fairliehope is reached—a little steading picturesquely situated on a height at the mouth of a steep-sided green glen that runs up into the recesses of Mount Maw. From this farm there is a tolerably good road to Carlops, which those may take who prefer easy walking, but the more picturesque way to Carlops is down the river-side. Cross the stile at Fairliehope, and follow the path that skirts the little garden, and then go straight down the hillside to the point where a couple of shaky logs bridge the North Esk water. The path after this is very narrow, and in some places rather steep; in damp weather it is also very slippery—I have seen people

* See p. 123.   † See p. 124.   ‡ See p. 123.

taking bits of it on all-fours *—but it is shorter than
the road, and leads through a prettier country. We
keep the left bank of the North Esk, which "burbles"
joyously down a deep glen. The scene is quietly beautiful. I have cast many a line upon this turbulent
stream with varying success. At no point above Carlops does it present insurmountable difficulties to a
good jumper, but in its rapid, broken waters there is
abundance of trout. Of no great size as a rule, but
now and again a good one has been taken, and possi-
bility is the chief nourishment of the angler's hopes.
The characteristics of the ravine through which we
pass are typical of the Pentland valleys. Few trees
are to be seen; of rock-scenery there is almost none;
little boldness of contour in the landscape; steep de-
clivities green from summit to base, where sheep
maintain an apparently impossible foothold; there are
imposing *rondeurs*, whose green melts into the greys,
browns, and purples of heath and ling; the whole
blending in a curious manner the suggestions of wildness and peacefulness. To me one of its greatest
charms is its glorious solitude. As the crow flies the
great city is scarcely twelve miles distant; as one

* One summer I descanted on the charm of this walk to two ladies
from Glasgow who were staying at West Linton. They went off together
to enjoy it, but returned from their walk mightly indignant because I had
not warned them of its perils. They told me they had ventured a few
hundred yards up the glen from Carlops at the risk of their lives, and, find-
ing the path more trying than Sauchiehall Street, had turned homeward
in disgust. The dangers of the expedition, in their view, consisted in the
extreme narrowness of the path, its alarming height above the river—
never more than 30 feet—and its painful slipperiness. The suggestion that
they should put nails in their dainty *bottines* was received with contumely.

feels it might be twelve thousand. You may pass a whole day there without seeing a single human soul, and the signs of human habitation are few and far between. The sight of the ruined mill and the sound of the waterfall * beside it warn us that we have come within eye-and-ear-shot of Carlops, and are over the range.

A few notes may be added about the path over the Spittal Hill. We cross the dam of the reservoir and ascend a steep path that makes for the pass between that hill and Patie's Hill. Just before we lose sight of the reservoir, turn and take a look at the glorious landscape behind us. To the south-west are seen in the blue distance the Tweedsmuir Hills; of the Pentlands, the top of Mendick is seen peeping over the shoulder of Mount Maw, at the foot of which is seen the serpentining valley of the North Esk; straight in front of us, across the reservoir, are the rounded summits of Deerhope Rig and The Mount, beyond which can be descried part of the West Cairn Hill acting as a dark background to the depression that separates The Mount from Wether Law; to the right of that again is the bleak and rugged outline of the East Cairn Hill, between which and us is the enclosing ridge of the Kitchen Moss swelling up into the round green top of Cock Rig.

Resuming our journey, we reach the summit of the pass in a few yards, from which point the descent is steep, but over agreeably soft turf, a fine view opening to our sight as we go down. To the left many of the summits of the North Central Mass appear in a

* See p. 51.

fore-shortened group. Beginning at the ridge of the Spittal Hill we identify the peaks in order as follows: the West Kip, Gap Law, Scald Law and South Black Hill, below which is the outline of the Monks' Rig, Braid Law and Pillar Knowe. To the right, nothing is visible but the shoulder of Patie's Hill. Below us, in front, is a large broad-shouldered knoll, with a sheep-fold a-top. Dod Hill,* beyond which again lie the little hamlet of Nine-Mile-Burn, and a magnificent expanse of moor, field and wood, to the Muirfoot Hills on the far horizon. The path soon skirts the banks of a pretty little burn that leaps merrily down the hill-side; and near the foot of Dod Hill, just above the Spittal farm, we pass a little pond which is scarcely a hundred yards from the conjectured site of the ancient *hospitium ;* which pond I more than half suspect to have been constructed by the monks of old to provide for their " fasting " on Fridays. The Spittal farm and its interesting features have already been described.†

2. *Balerno to Carlops* viâ *Marchbank and the Bore-Stane* (9 *miles*).

This is a pleasant variation of the walk just indicated. With the exception of two miles, it has been already described. As far as Marchbank the route is the same as on p. 114. Beyond Marchbank, instead of going down to Redford and the reservoir, we take the road to the right, an old cart-road that goes

* See p. 122, *note*. † See p. 123.

straight to Listonshiels,* where we join the pathway leading over the hills.

3. *Mid-Calder to Carlops* viâ *the Bore Stane* (9¾ *miles*).

Mid-Calder station is on the Caledonian main line from Edinburgh. On leaving the train, we turn to the left, and make for Kirknewton village, keeping to the right as we pass it, whence we hold straight on, with fine stretches of woodland on both sides, to the Lanark road. Here we turn to the left, and walk towards Edinburgh for nearly three-quarters of a mile, until we reach the side road going by Haugh Head farm towards Listonshiels, as described above.†

* See p. 127.   † See p. 127.

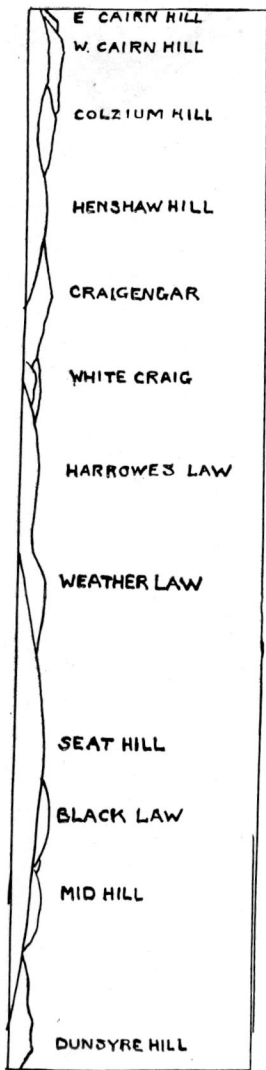

A.

E CAIRN HILL
W. CAIRN HILL
COLZIUM HILL
HENSHAW HILL
CRAIGENGAR
WHITE CRAIG
HARROWES LAW
WEATHER LAW
SEAT HILL
BLACK LAW
MID HILL
DUNSYRE HILL

B.

BLACK HILL
(or Dolphinton)
DUNSYRE
TINTO
CORBIES' CRAIGS
DUNSYRE HILL
MID HILL
BLACK LAW
MEDWYNHEAD
BLACK HILL

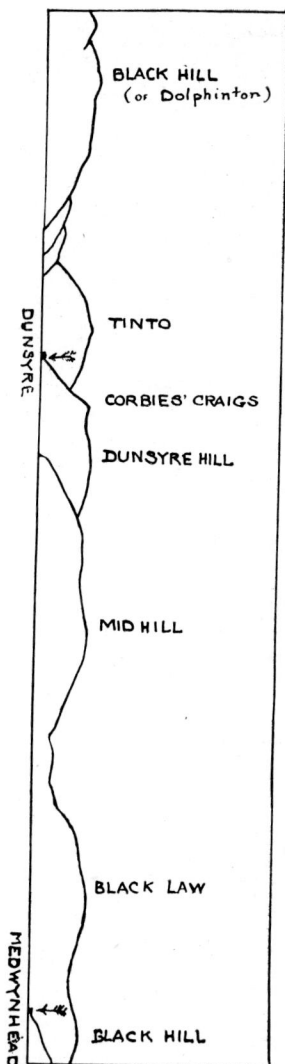

South Mass, as seen from
A.—Easter Yardhouse
B.—Slipperfield Mount

[*To face page* 136

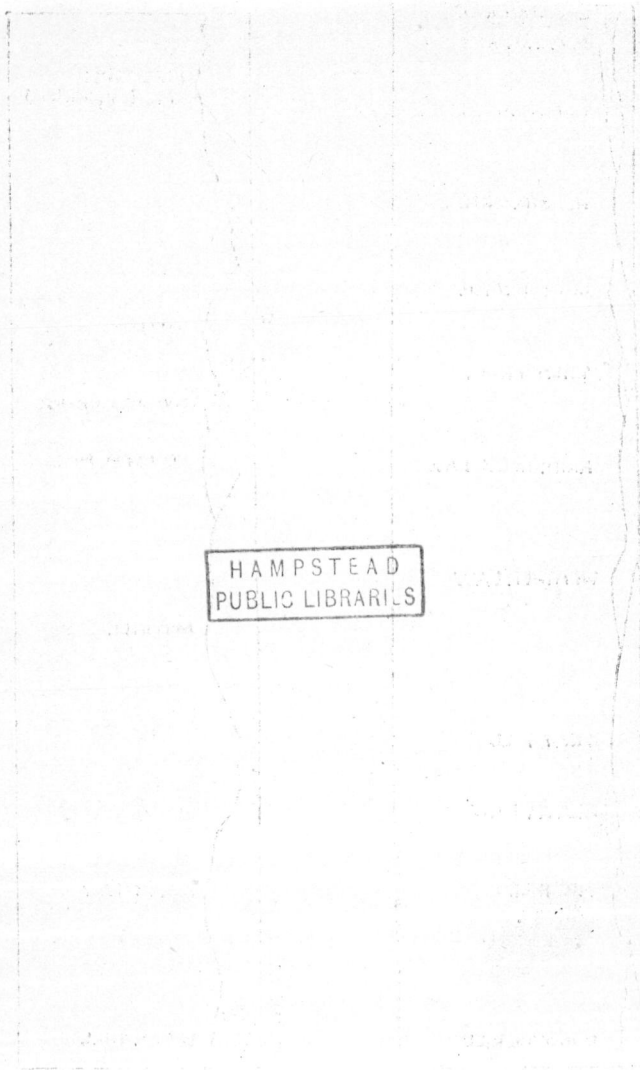

CHAPTER XV

WALKS ACROSS THE SOUTH MASS

THE walks across the South Mass of the Pentlands are longer, and in some respects more varied and interesting, than those touched upon in the previous chapters. And of the longer tramps across the range there is none better known, or more appreciated, than that between Mid-Calder and West Linton by the Cauldstane Slap. Indeed, when the average citizen of Edinburgh hears one talk about a walk across the Pentlands, he makes some tentative allusion to Glencorse or the Cauldstane Slap, occasionally confounding the two; which fact shows that light is dawning, if slowly, on the inhabitants of the capital.

The principal starting-points for this district are Mid-Calder, Harburn and Auchengray, all stations on the Caledonian main line to Carlisle.

1. *Mid-Calder to West Linton* viâ *the Cauldstane Slap* (12 *miles*).

From Mid-Calder Station we first hold westward for a few hundred yards until a sign-post intimates that our way is to the left. A fairly straight and shady road leads us past Belstane farm to the Lanark road, which we follow in a south-westerly direction for three-quarters of a mile, passing first, on the right,

Aimville, which is as Frenchy in appearance as in name, for it looks like an old Normandy farmhouse, and then, on the left, the ruins of Little Vantage inn. At the old Toll House, just beyond, we see another sign-post intimating that our way is to the left. Down by the side of a copse, we take what path we can find to the Water of Leith, where stepping-stones of uncertain stability enable us to cross dry-shod, if the stream be not in flood. Harper Rig reservoir* lies on our right as we cross, and the farm of the same name is in front. Passing that, we have to plod for a mile or two over heathery wastes and bogs, with no distinctly marked track, though the posts indicate the line of an old drove road connecting the still famous Falkirk Tryst with the almost forgotten Linton market. The tramp in some places is very heavy, especially if the weather is not, or has not recently been, dry; but the air and the scenery and the resultant vigour are worth all the toil and tribulation of the journey. The track— such as it is—keeps fairly close to the course of the Baad Park burn, which is a considerable feeder of Harper Rig. The stiffest bit of the climb is when we approach the source of that stream, and scramble up the ridge, which, like a curtain between bastions, connects the two Cairn Hills. The summit of the pass, which is called the Cauldstane Slap,† is 1435 feet

---

* See p. 93. If by reason of flood the stepping-stones are not negotiable, the Water of Leith can be crossed higher up, in the neighbourhood of the reservoir.

† "Slap" means a permanent opening in a dyke through which sheep and cattle may pass—generally with no gate attached. A gate that lies open, however, may be in the slap. It is here used figuratively to describe this narrow pass in the hills.

above sea-level. The origin of the name Cauldstane
I have been unable to ascertain. There are boulders
enough and to spare scattered about the pass, and
they are " cauld " enough in all conscience, for, as a
rule, one meets a fine cutting wind on these heights,
but I scarcely think this fact explains the name.*
There are in the neighbourhood, outcrops of red sandstone, about the size of an ordinary dining-table—
which have been used for *al fresco* lunches by not a few
pedestrians—and these may account for the name.
A farm called " Cauldstaneslap " appears in *Weir of
Hermiston*, and though the editor of that unfinished
romance declares that it is impossible to guess where
Stevenson places the scene of his story, I have the
temerity to believe that all the materials of it lie in
or near the Pentlands. I think Stevenson had the real
Cauldstane Slap in his mind, but, with the romancer's
license, took the liberty of lifting it, body-bulk, some
eight miles to the north-eastward. If not, then he
shifted old Glencorse parish church as far to the
south-westward. Further, his magic wand transported
the Covenanter's grave from the Black Hill and
planted it in the middle of the Slap. This is a mere
guess, of course, but those who know the Pentlands,
and have also read *Weir of Hermiston* carefully, will recognise how the suggested combination of scenes suits
the story. Authors, however, dramatise their narratives
amid scenery that is a mosaic of many landscapes.

* In Timothy Pont's map the name is spelled "Coldstounstopp"; in
letters from the Committee of the Privy Council to General Dalzell and
to various Peeblesshire lairds (1666) it appears as "Colstounslope."

Very wild and sombre is the Slap, and if the day be grey, as it so often is in our brumous isle, and if the clouds are flying low, scraping the sides of the hills, it looks desolate in the extreme. We are miles away from the nearest human habitation. Looking northward from the ridge, we have a view whose soft beauties are in strong contrast to the bleak ruggedness of our immediate surroundings. Below our feet the ground falls away abruptly to the broad muir that forms the northern fringe of the Pentlands, beyond which the Lothians, the winding Forth, the hills of Stirling, Perth and Fife, enchant our vision. The Slap is on the boundary between Midlothian and Peeblesshire, in which latter county lies all the rest of our walk. High on the western side of the gorge, at the foot of which runs the Lyne Water, the path, now clearly visible, keeps along the side of the West Cairn Hill as far as the Ravendean burn. Up this glen to the right, surely safe enough from the attentions of the dreaded dragoons, conventicles used to be held by the Covenanters in the dark days of the persecution.* A fine screen of hills shuts in the valley of the Lyne on its eastern side, these being in order, Wether Law, The Mount and Mount Maw (with a high ridge between the last two). On the other side there is the heavy mass of Byrehope Mount and the graceful pyramid of Kingseat.

At Baddingsgill,† opposite the shooting-lodge of

---

* In *Frae the Lyne Valley*, by Robert Sanderson, there is a poem on the Ravendean burn. See p. 47, *note*.

† *i.e.* Baldwin's Gill (or hill). In Timothy Pont's map Baddingsgill, Slipperfield and the Cauldstane Slap are all placed in "Clydsdail."

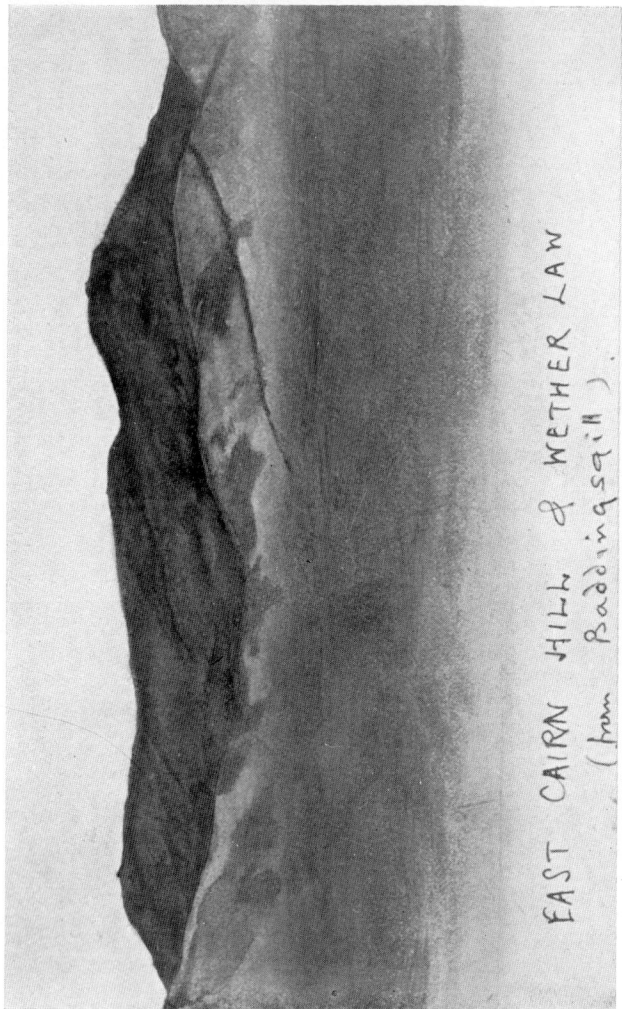

EAST CAIRN HILL & WETHER LAW
(from Baddingsgill).

Drummond Young & Watson

(From a Water-Colour Sketch by the Author)

[Edinburgh]

[To face page 140]

Cairnmuir, the track becomes a tolerable road. The
Lyne Water pursues a wonderfully sinuous course
in the valley below; its channel reminds one of the
cañons of Colorado on a small scale, as do many of
the sykes in the neighbourhood.* This water was
once a great favourite with anglers; it is still patronised by them—the fishing is open—but, alas, it is not
now up to its former reputation! Possibly, however,
the reputation of a trout-stream owes more to the imagination than to the experience of those who lament
the glories of a bygone day.

When we emerge from the narrower path of the
valley upon the open moorland, a panorama of great
extent and singular beauty unrolls itself to the view.
The main features of this have been already indicated.†
A mile or so more, and we are on the shady road between Medwyn House and the Linton golf-course,
which takes us by an easy descent to the village,
which has abundant (mercenary) hospitality for all
comers. Broomlee station, on the North British system, is three-quarters of a mile further on.

Though not in any real sense a heavy tramp, this is
probably the heaviest on the Pentlands so far as the
rights-of-way are concerned. One certainly has a new
respect for the Pentlands after doing this journey for
the first time. You respect your difficulties when you
have surmounted them. If you despise them they will
take a mean revenge. Some men I have known, in
spite of warnings from the well-informed, have taken
bicycles with them on this expedition. For eight miles

* See p. 128, *note*.   † See p. 59.

out of the twelve, their sufferings were unspeakable
and their language unprintable. Once upon a time—
it was before 1900—a United Presbyterian minister
in West Lothian waxed eloquent to a friend on the
glories of this excursion, advised him to try it, and
assured him that there was a fairly good road all the
way. Like a familiar class of moralists, he urged his
friend to go a way he had never taken himself, and
had no mind to. The credulous friend started gaily one
morning—in a dog-cart. The shades of night were
falling when there limped into West Linton, leading a
broken-kneed horse, which dragged wearily behind it
a load of ostensible fire-wood on two wheels and a
twisted axle, a way-worn traveller, who was under-
stood to say, in short intervals between long blas-
phemies, that during the journey he had completely
lost his faith in man.

2. *Newpark to West Linton* viâ *the Cauldstane Slap*
(13½ *miles*).

This is not a route that Edinburgh pedestrians are
likely to take, but it deserves mention here. Newpark
is a station on the Caledonian Railway between Edinburgh and Glasgow, at which only the slower trains
stop.

Leaving the station, take the road going southward
for a mile and a half; then follow the by-road to the
left that crosses the Linhouse Water, goes eastward
between Corston and Auchinoon Hills, and joins the
Lanark road opposite the old Toll-House, whence

starts the path to the Cauldstane Slap described above.

3. *Balerno to West Linton* viâ *the Cauldstane Slap*.

There are three ways of doing this. (1) By taking the Lanark road from Balerno station to the old Toll-House, and proceeding as above (13¼ miles); (2) By going to Listonshiels, as described on p. 142, and thence taking a bee-line across the moor to East Cairn Hill (about 14 miles); (3) By going to Listonshiels *viâ* Marchbank, as shown on p. 135, and taking the same bee-line (about 13 miles). The bee-line is, of course, not a right-of-way, and, moreover, it is very heavy walking in parts.

4. *Harburn to Dunsyre, Dolphinton or West Linton* viâ *Henshaw Hill*.

On leaving, Harburn station, we hold south-westward for a quarter of a mile until we join the road connecting West Calder with the Lanark road, and turn to the left at that point. We are soon passing, on the hillside to the left, " Cromwell's Stone," and the remains of a camp which the Lord Protector occupied for a time when he was invading central Scotland after the battle of Dunbar. Little more than a mile further on, as we cross the shoulder of Camilty Hill, is the site of a Roman camp, evidence of an older, and perhaps more successful, invasion. Reaching the Lanark road, almost opposite the Crosswood reser-

voir,* we turn to the right, and keep on till we see a
post on the left directing us to the hills. Here there is
a cart-road leading towards the reservoir, half-way to
which another post indicates the line we take—which
is straight across the moor and up the slope of Henshaw Hill, slightly to the left of the top. Henshaw is a
broad, round, flat-topped hill whose ascent is easy.
Just beyond the gate in the dry-stane dyke (which
dyke, by the way, is here the boundary between Midlothian and Lanarkshire) stands another post, where
the alleged path from Auchengray joins our present
one. This post points with cheery vagueness to the
whole semi-circle of the horizon on our right, and remarks, by means of an embossed inscription on an iron
plate, " Public Path to West Linton and Dunsyre."
The statement is manifestly ironical, for nothing even
remotely resembling a path have I found on that wild
waste of stone and heather. It is very easy to lose
one's way here, for there is not a post to guide us for
two miles, and therefore the pedestrian has to " ca'
canny." Thus care should be taken not to miss the right
line. It is the same as that we have taken since leaving
Crosswood (S.S.E.), but the three valleys or sykes below
are somewhat confusing. We keep straight on, then, in
this line down to the Garval Syke, where the South
Medwyn Water takes its rise. We now have a stiff
climb of nearly four hundred feet in less than a quarter
of a mile, to the left of the summit of the White Craig,
and on gaining more level ground keep along past the
rocky Darlees Rig on our right. The view now in front

* See p. 93.

Drummond Young & Watson]　　　　　　　　　　　[Edinburgh

THE COVENANTER'S GRAVE

(From a Painting by James Kinnear, exhibited in the Royal Scottish Academy, 1909)

[To face page 144

of us, as the country opens out to our sight, is rather
like a choppy sea solidified at the moment of its
greatest restlessness: it is a wonderfully varied panorama. The path leads us down past the Black Hill *
to the valley of the West Water,† but no one should
leave the Black Hill without paying a visit of curiosity, or of sympathy, to the Covenanter's grave. To
reach this, we have to scramble up the hillside, where,
near the top, in a lonely and stony waste, stands a grey
slab bearing this inscription: " Sacred to the memory
of a Covenanter who fought and was wounded
at Rullion Green, November 28, 1666, and who died
at Oakenbush the day after the Battle and was buried
here by Adam Sanderson of Blackhill." The tradition,
as I got it piecemeal from various local people, ran
thus: At dead of night, on 28th November 1666, Adam
Sanderson, tenant of Blackhill farm,‡ was wakened
by a tapping at his window. He rose to find a poor
fugitive covered with mud and bloodstains, who
begged his assistance. He had taken part in the desperate fight at Rullion Green that day, and had fled
wounded from the scene. Sanderson would have taken
him in, at the risk of severe penalties for harbouring
a wild Whig, but the man would not accept hospitality so dangerous to his host. The two went together
up the valley of the Westwater, but ere long the

* Often but erroneously called the Black Law. The real Black Law is
a hill to the south-west of this (1460 ft.).

† This stream, a tributary of the South Medwyn, must not be confounded with another of the same name some miles further to the east, a tributary of the Lyne. (See p. 61, *note*).

‡ See p. 151.

K

fugitive sank down exhausted, and expired in Sanderson's arms, his last words being, " Bury me in sight of the Ayrshire hills." The farmer carried the dead man to the top of the Black Hill, and buried him there, marking the spot with a small cairn. The erection of the present slab was occasioned by an unexpected confirmation of the old legend. The story, as I first received it, was this: that an enterprising youth, a farmer's son in the Easton district, went to the top of the hill with a spade, with a view to discovering whether tradition was correct in declaring that this spot was the Covenanter's grave. He began to dig, and speedily found what he was after. He came home in triumph with a skull, some pieces of cloth, and a few brass buttons; but his father, a true-blue Presbyterian, indignant at the desecration of a spot hallowed to the mind of every patriotic Scotsman, first administered a severe thrashing to his son, and then went with him to re-inter the sacred relics where Adam Sanderson had laid the remains of the poor fugitive long before. It was then resolved to mark the spot with a permanent monument.* (The name of this

* I take the liberty of printing some extracts from an article written in the *Weekly Scotsman* (1907) by Mr P. F. Dunlop, who resides at Dolphinton, and who is a man both deeply interested and well informed in regard to local antiquities. He quotes the following from *Blackwood's Magazine* for October 1817 :—" On the farm of Easton, in the parish of Dunsyre, a tradition has been handed down from father to son in a family who as shepherds have resided in the place for many generations back, that a certain rude stone set up in an adjoining moor marked the grave of one of the covenanters, who, having been wounded at the battle fought at the Pentland Hills, died of his wounds on his way home, and was buried by the great-grandfather of the person from whom we have the tradition. Accordingly, a few days ago, several persons, desirous to ascer-

Covenanter has been ascertained to be John Car-
phin.)

Descending to our path again, and coming round
the shoulder of the Black Hill, we descry the ruins of
Adam Sanderson's little farmhouse down by the

tain the truth of this story, went to the place, and having dug about two
feet below the surface found the remains of a decayed skeleton. A medical gentleman, Dr Black (of Biggar, a brother of Hugh Black, who opened
the grave), who was on the spot, could distinguish one of the thigh-bones,
which was almost entire in shape, though reduced nearly to the consist-
ence of the mossy soil which surrounded it. The scalp was found complete, covered with very long hair of a whiteish colour nearly as fresh and
strong as in life ; several fragments of clothes were also found, among
which some leather buttons were plainly discernible. In addition to the
above were found two silver coins, weighing about one ounce each, bearing the date 1620, and having on one side the following inscription :—
' *Belg. Gel. Mo. Arg. Pro. Confœ.*, with the following sentence on the
other :—*Concordia Res Parvœ Crescunt.*' From the state of the coins
there is reason to believe that they had been sewed or tied up closely in
some part of the wearer's clothes. It must have been upwards of 138 years
since the body of this poor covenanter was committed to his lonely grave."
Mr Dunlop then proceeds—" I have taken the trouble to interview several persons born in the neighbourhood and intimately acquainted with
the tradition. My first informant says that the covenanter was wounded
at Rullion Green ; that he wandered west along the Pentlands; and that
he arrived at Blackhill farm (erroneously called Black Law in the Survey map), situated on the S.E. . . . of Blackhill, close to the south Med-
win. The ruins of the house are still to be seen, and in the remaining gable
a small window, now built up, is pointed out as that to which the covenanter came in the dead of night. He did not wish to be taken into the house,
as he knew that the dragoons would be in search of fugitives, and as he
was mortally wounded he expressed a wish that he might be buried in
sight of the Ayrshire hills. . . . Adam Sanderson, the farmer of Blackhill,
did everything he could for his comfort, and then conveyed him up the
course of the West Water to a stunted oak bush in a sheltered spot, where
he died. His wish was faithfully carried out by the said Adam Sanderson,
who buried him where the present tombstone stands, in sight of the Ayrshire hills. As he was buried near the top of the Black Hill, which is 1336
feet high, and as there is a gap through the hills to the N. of Black Law,
erroneously called in the maps Bleak Law, it is quite possible to see hills

water-side to the left. We then cross the drove road
between West Linton and Auchengray,* and hold
athwart the green and somewhat boggy moor that
separates the Westwater from the South Medwyn.
When our path strikes the Westwater, it divides, the
left-hand track going down the burnside towards the
confluence of the two streams, crossing the South
Medwyn—and also the Lanark-Peebles boundary—
by a foot-bridge, passing Garvald House, and reaching the Biggar road at Dolphinton station (Caledonian); † the right-hand one leading us over the Westwater and taking us by a wood and a pond—or tarn—
whence we see Easton farm ‡ lying below us. From
Easton we can go by the farm-road, or take the short
cut down the burn side, to Dunsyre village.§

in Ayrshire about eighteen miles 'as the crow flies.' Tradition says that
part of the woollen cloth found in the grave was washed ; that its colour
was a dull red ; that the two silver coins found in the grave were 'clipped'
and that they found their way to the British Museum ; that the skull was
taken by some sacrilegious person to Easton, where it was not too rever-
ently treated ; that the covenanter's body was twice buried, first by the
side of the West Water and afterwards in its present position. A native of
Dunsyre states that Hugh Black, son of the farmer in Easton, opened the
grave one evening ; that while intently occupied in doing so his collie,
which had gone after a hare, came panting up behind him and jumped on
his back ; that Hugh was so scared that he made for home as hard as he
could run ; that it was on the day thereafter that he and several others
returned to complete the examination of the grave ; that it was at the in-
stigation of Dr Manuel, minister of Dunsyre, and mainly at his expense,
that the tombstone was set up about the year 1841."

This is an interesting variation of the legend.

* See p. 156. Here we walk by faith, not by sight, for the guide-posts
have been removed.

† The distance from Harburn to this point is 11½ miles.

‡ See p. 146, *note*.

§ See p. 80. The distance from Harburn to Dunsyre by this route is
about 11 miles.

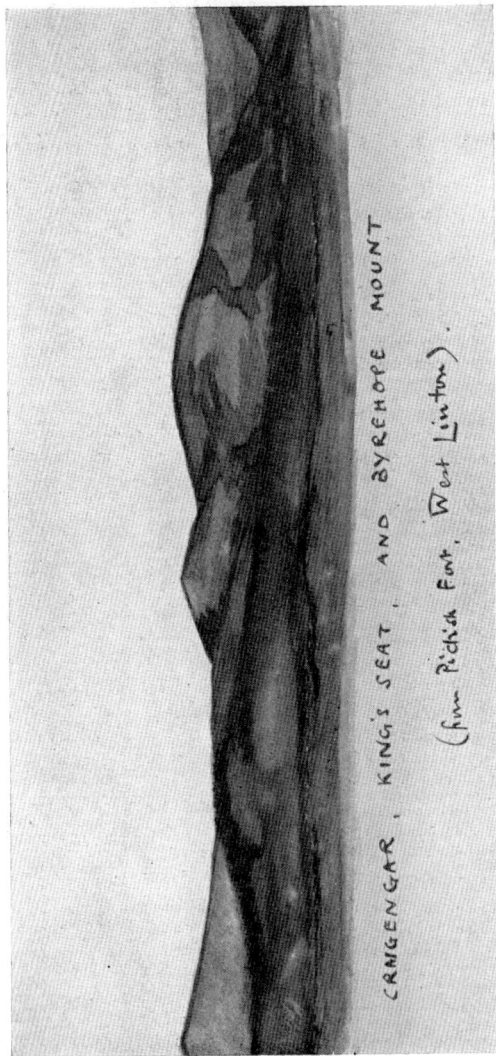

CRAIGENGAR, KING'S SEAT, AND BYREHOPE MOUNT

(from Pictish Fort, West Linton).

Drummond Young & Watson]

(From a Water-Colour Sketch by the Author)

[Edinburgh

[To face page 148

To reach West Linton by this route we turn to the left on the drove road already mentioned, go down into the valley of the South Medwyn, cross the stream opposite Medwynhead, a shepherd's house which a famous Scottish artist, Mr John Faed, has made his retreat, and then hold our way across a wide bleak moor, with Mendick's characteristic outline in front of us—slightly to the right—and with Craigengar,* Byrehope Mount and Kingseat on the left. The best time of year to take this route is either in winter under a hard frost, or in summer after a long drought: at other times and seasons it can be very sloppy indeed. The path skirts for a mile the bed of a stream ironically called the Dry burn. I have never seen it dry, save with that kind of dryness which frost creates, but, to judge from the wetness of the pathway, I should accuse it of neglecting its duty as a natural drain. We cross the eastern Westwater (or Polintarf) by a footbridge near North Slipperfield farm, whence we tramp gaily towards West Linton—downhill most of the way—either across the golf-course, or round it, by the road that passes Medwyn House.†

The route to West Linton, however, can be very agreeably varied by leaving the right-of-way on the alleged path on Henshaw Hill and going down the valley direct to Medwynhead. To do this make for the wall beyond the post mentioned on p. 144, and follow it down to the Garval Syke, to the point where

* There is a cave in this hill "said to have been a chief rendezvous of gipsies or tinkers in this part of the country."—*New Statistical Account*.

† See p. 58.

the three gullies meet. The White Craig and the Pike are in front, the former to the right and the latter to the left. Two small streams meet where the wall reaches the bottom of the depression: that on the right is the South Medwyn Water, whose course is now to be the line of our tramp. A quarter of a mile on, between the Pike and Millstone Rig, a streamlet coming from Craigengar joins the Medwyn, and the confluence marks the meeting of three counties. One may have the unusual sensation of being in three counties at once by straddling the streamlet, and putting his stick on the opposite bank of the Medwyn; he will thus have the singular pleasure of knowing that his right foot is in Midlothian, his left in Peeblesshire, while his stick is resting on the soil of Lanarkshire. The only risk one runs in assuming this strange geographical attitude is that of getting wet feet.

All the surroundings of the Medwyn in this district are picturesque; the walk down its banks is easy and delightful. The angler's eye looks with interest on its many deep, rocky pools, and its long, turbulent rushes, suggestive of lusty trout. The fishing here is open, but of late years it has not been very good. In spring the water, when it is low, is almost unfishable, owing to the accumulation of green slime. A mile below the geographical point mentioned above, we pass, on the right bank of the stream, a heap of stones known as Roger's Kirk. This marks a spot where conventicles were held in the days when Covenanters were being hunted on the hills, and is believed to take its name from a covenanting minister

who preached there. Nearly another mile below this
we come upon the ruins of Blackhill farm * with a
few thin trees keeping them company, and on the opposite side of the river the cottage of Medwynhead,
whence we make for West Linton across the moor as
indicated above, p. 149.†

5. *Auchengray to Dunsyre, Dolphinton or West Linton* viâ *Henshaw Hill.*

Auchengray station suggests memories of Robert,
or " Bob " as he was familiarly called, for eighteen
years a soldier, and for thirty-three a porter here.
His wild yell of agony in announcing the name of the
station made not a few passengers jump on their seats
under the impression that somebody had been run
over. " Bob " has gone to his rest, and is greatly
missed by all who knew him. We hold northward
from the station for a little more than a mile, and
then, taking the first road to the right, keep east-
wards for three miles by a route which, though uninteresting in itself, being a plain country road, yet
being a gentle ascent towards the outworks of the
Pentlands, commands rather extensive views. When
we reach the Lanark road we simply cross it to the
post at the other side, and then make for Henshaw
Hill, by a moorland path, which, after the first few
hundred yards, would require the keen sight of a Red

* See pp. 145 *et seq.*

† The distance between Harburn and West Linton by this route is rather more than 12 miles.

Indian tracker to discover it. We keep by the right
shoulder of Henshaw Hill to the point where the am-
biguous sign-post marks the meeting of our present
path with that from Harburn, and from this the route
is the same as described on p. 144.*

6. *Auchengray to West Linton* viâ *Left Law and Dunsyre.*

For this walk we take the road southward from
Auchengray village past Muirhall farm, to a cart-
road leading to the left, which brings us first to King's
Inns † farm, and then to Easter Yardhouse. From
the latter point the road becomes a turfy track over a
wide bleak moor, and it reaches the North Medwyn
Water at a rather deep ford. A few yards down the
stream there is a plank-bridge by which we may cross
dry-shod if the water is low, but as the plank does not
stretch from bank to bank—only to a little stony
beach on the other side—it is somewhat difficult to
negotiate the crossing when the stream is in spate.‡
Up the hillside, on the Lang Whang, lie the ruins of
Boston Cottage, which once marked a stage on the
road between Edinburgh and Lanark. We cross the

* The distances are :—Auchengray to Dolphinton, or Dunsyre, about
11 miles ; and to West Linton, about 12.

† The name of this farm is said to be derived from the fact that one of
the Scottish kings paused there once, or that several Scottish kings were
in the habit of pausing there, amid the ardour of the chase, for rest and
refreshment.   There is a well of very fine water close by.

‡ Since this was written a rough bridge of logs has been built a few
yards above the ford, by Mr Warrack of Kersewell.

road, and should see a post indicating the path over the hills, but we don't. The right-of-way posts in this district have been taken down by the local laird, who presumably desires that pedestrians should walk anyhow and everyhow over his land instead of keeping strictly to the right-of-way. Otherwise it is hard to account for his action. The path, going straight up the hill opposite Boston Cottage, leads over a slope of the Lingy Knowe, up Seat Hill, from which point there is a very extensive view to the north and west, very mossy and heathery in the foreground, but enriched with woodland, hill and field beyond. Between the summit of Seat Hill and Weather Law, which faces us to the east, two little green knolls stand side by side called the Twin Laws, near a small sheet of water, a mere tarn, which is dignified by the name of the Crane Loch. The path above described, however, is not a right-of-way.

The proper path goes slightly to the right towards a gate in the fence, and thenceforward for a considerable distance is fairly well marked. We are here skirting the end of the Pentlands, the bleak and boggy moorland into which the hills gradually sink. Crossing the Westruther burn, the path holds up the shoulder of the Left Law (1181 feet), where, just beyond a gate in a march-dyke, it meets the drove road from Medwynhead.* From this point there is a splendid outlook, embracing not only the south-western end of the range and the Black Hill of Dolphinton, but also the hills of Tweedsmuir, Clydesdale and Annan-

* See p. 149.

dale. Our route now keeps almost due south, past
Stonypath—probably so-called because of an old
Roman road in the neighbourhood—to the road between Newbigging and Dunsyre,* a little to the west
of Anston, whence a walk of less than a mile brings us
to Dunsyre, beyond which we take the road to the
left leading at some distance past Easton farm, and
thence downwards to the Westwater, which we cross
a few yards above its junction with the South Medwyn. On the tongue of land at the confluence the
Romans once had a fortified outpost—a situation, as
one may see, admirably suited for defence. We keep
on a footpath on the north side of the Medwyn Water
for a quarter of a mile, cross the latter by a foot-
bridge—there is a ford here also for vehicular traffic
—between Medwynbank and Fernyhaugh,† and
thence take the cart-road past the farm up the hillside to the left along the north side of a pretty
wood.

After a climb of about a hundred feet, the path

* See p. 80 *et seq.*

† The road to the right going down to a white gate is the route to Dolphinton stations and the Biggar road, a pleasing variation of the journey
to West Linton. Especially pleasing is the route by the old road, past Ingraston farm, and thence over a surface of green turf along the south
side of Mendick Hill. Near this road, according to Captain Armstrong, in
his *Companion to the Map of Tweeddale*, there were discovered, before
1775, "several entombed bodies of gigantic stature, and thought (*sic*)
to have been the burial-place of some distinguished heroes or sacred persons." The road passes through some shady plantations behind Slipperfield Loch, which, however, is not visible here, to South Slipperfield
farm, whence we can go to West Linton, either straight through the wood
over the old bridge (p. 61), and past the golf-course, or by turning to
the right and making for the Edinburgh road.

Drummond Young & Watson] [*Edinburgh*

DUNSYRE HILL AND THE CORBIES' CRAIGS

[*To face page* 154.

goes straight towards the north-east, between the North Muir Hill (1175 feet) and Mendick, crossing a wide mossy plain on which are conspicuous, to the left, two large cairns, supposed to mark the site of a battle which history has forgotten. It is believed that the cairns, which are half a mile apart, commemorate the slain on the two sides. On the right, there is a steep, almost precipitous slope to a narrow valley, seamed and scarred in all directions with drainage channels, at the bottom of which there winds, like a long, thin, wriggling worm, the Garvald burn. Almost abreast of the upper cairn, we cross the watershed between the Lyne and the South Medwyn. From the moor we have just crossed, looking backwards— *i.e.* westwards—we have a magnificent view of the Lanarkshire portion of the South Mass. In front is the jagged outline of Dunsyre Hill with the Corbies' Craigs, the rounded outline of the Mid Hill, the dark shoulder of the Black Hill, while to the right is the long, flattened pyramid of Craigengar. To the south rise the imposing heights of the Black Hill of Dolphinton, often called the Black Mount. Facing northwards again, and crossing the watershed near the upper cairn, we see, about twenty feet below us on the right, a little spring coming bubbling out of the hillside, amid a cluster of stones, whose arrangement seems to be partly natural and partly artificial. This is the source of the Garvald burn, named on maps and in guide-books the Rumbling Well, but popularly known as " Thirsty Katie." We now descend into a flat saucer-shaped valley, striped like a zebra with drains,

and thence over a ridge into the valley of the alleged
Dry burn,* beyond which we see near a wood a sign-
post marking the junction of our present route with
that described on p. 149.

7. *West Linton to Auchengray* viâ *Medwynhead.*

The road between West Linton and Medwynhead
has already been described. It is an old drove road,
which means that it is often anything but well marked.
It is conventionally considered to be forty yards
broad, and the multiplicity of trails leading apparently in all directions amongst the heather is apt to be
confusing. From Medwynhead we cross the stream
and make the best guess we can at the path, taking a
bee-line over the Cairn Knowe to the Westwater
valley. The posts marked on the pedestrian's map are
non-existent. Scrambling down the steep bank of the
Westwater, and up the opposite side, we have a toilsome ascent, not very steep, but long and awfully
boggy, to the pass between the summits of the Mid
Hill and the Black Law. I think that the walk between the Cairn Knowe and this pass is one of the
wettest in the Pentlands. It is not a journey to
be taken by the young gentlemen friends of the
recent newspaper correspondent who wished stepping-
stones laid across the bogs of the Pentlands, because
the young men of to-day dislike getting their boots
soiled. From the summit of the pass we descend,

* See p. 149.

having before us a magnificent view to the west, to
the gate in the dyke, near which our path joins that
between Boston Cottage and Stonypath.* We turn to
the right, make our way to Auchengray station, and
so home.

* See p. 154.

CHAPTER XVI

SHORTER WALKS

SOME brief indication should be given of a few shorter walks about the hills, starting from various centres, demanding less time for their accomplishment, and suited—like the Shorter Catechism—to " such as are of weaker capacity."

1. *Swanston to the top of Caerketton or Allermuir.*

There is a steep path from the village of Swanston up the gully between Caerketton and Allermuir, which keeps the line of the barbed-wire fence near the little streamlet that comes down the hillside. Near the beginning of this path there are notices strictly prohibiting the public from walking on the grounds of Swanston farm, but as they give no information as to which are the lands alluded to they may be disregarded, so far as this path is concerned. The walk is steep and trying to the short-winded, but for a great part of the way it is over soft and springy turf, very pleasant to the tread, and the view attained on reaching the top of either hill is worth a heavier output of energy. The nearer summit is that of Caerketton, a long ridge running from east to west, crowned by two cairns, the easterly one marking the highest point of the hill. From this point the Caerketton Craigs do not look so steep as from the foot, and the real conformation of the so-called " T-Plantation " becomes visible. This wood is actually cruciform, but the centre of the cross is at the top of a knoll called the White Hill, and its four arms are planted down the sides towards the principal points of the compass, so that from any point of view, except from above, the plantation appears to be T-shaped. Various explanations are given as to the origin of this manifestly artificial phenomenon. Some say that it was designed by one of the Trotters of Mortonhall to celebrate the marriage of a daughter, while others allege that it was an unsuccessful attempt to grow an anchor-shaped wood in commemoration of Nelson's victory at Trafalgar. From the summit of Allermuir a glorious view of the Logan valley is to be had, and also of the greater part of the range, not to mention the very extensive outlook over the valley of the Forth to the Highland hills, and down the Firth to the German Ocean, and southward over the beautifully-wooded Esk valleys to the Lammermuirs and Muirfoots.* From many a point on this north-eastern ridge we may " view yon Empress of the North sit on her hilly throne." And right royally she sits there.†

* From the top of Allermuir one may take a bee-line for the gate in the march-dyke mentioned on p. 108, and so over Fala Knowe to Castlelaw, and thence to Glencorse.

† It was possibly hereabouts that the Gibbites (or "Sweet Singers"), a little party of about thirty fanatics, mostly women, encamped for a few days in full view of the city to watch its destruction, after the manner of

2. *Logan Valley to Penicuik or Glencorse by Turnhouse Hill.*

Another very pretty walk, also somewhat trying to the short-winded, may be taken from a point about half-way between Loganlee and Glencorse reservoirs, nearly opposite the ruins of Logan Tower, up the burn that comes down from Caernethy towards the pass between that hill and its neighbour, Turnhouse. The pass is nearly 1500 feet above sea-level; the descent on the eastern side is very steep, but the magnificent panorama that opens to the sight at the top holds the eye fascinated to the danger of the feet. As there is not a right-of-way one is free, at his own risk, to take any line he chooses to the high road; but perhaps the most interesting line is past an old Pictish fort and the Covenanters' grave, and then across the battle-field of Rullion Green to Martyrs' Cross.* Thence to Penicuik or Glencorse, according to choice.

3. *West Linton, Cairn Muir and the Windy Gowl.*

A pleasant and easy walk can be taken from West

Sodom and Gomorrah, for its desperate wickedness (1681). The leader of the sect, John Gib, was a mariner belonging to Bo'ness. He and his party, as a religious body, did not survive a short term of imprisonment with hard labour inflicted by the authorities. Historians and annalists are irritatingly vague in their allusions to the Pentlands. So also is Oliver Cromwell, who dates several of his letters from his camp in the hills, but gives no indication of its exact site. Many believe that the scriptural names in the Morningside district of Edinburgh—Eden, Canaan, Jordan, etc.—were given by Cromwell's soldiers to a region which, with its rolling heights studded with stately old trees, and watered by a network of rivulets, must have seemed an earthly paradise to these English invaders.

* See p. 26.

ON THE LYNE (WEST LINTON)

(From a Photograph kindly sent by Mr E. J. Bedford, Eastbourne)

[To face page 160

Linton to the entrance of the Cairn Muir, then across the Lyne and over a ridge of Faw Mount, which is a spur of Mount Maw, to Stoneypath farm, whence to West Linton by the steep cart-road that leads down to the Gordon Arms Hotel. To do this walk take the golf-course road past Medwyn House,* and hold straight on past Wakefield to a post a few yards short of a foot-bridge that spans the Ely burn; thence go downwards to the right, cross the river to a post visible on the opposite side, whence there is a good track to Stoneypath in one direction, and to Cairnmuir shooting-lodge in the other.

From this road one may enter—there is no definite path—that curious sword-cut in the hills called the Windy Gowl, and can walk the whole length of it as far as Carlops. The conformation of the landscape here makes this a most interesting walk, though it is marshy in places.†

4. *Carnwath and back* viâ *Redford Bridge and Newbigging*.

This is an easy tramp, the first part being along the Edinburgh road past the entrance to Kersewell House and Parkneuk, into the North Medwyn valley. Crossing Redford bridge, we hold over the moor to the right, passing the south-western end of the wood we see facing us, and thence keep in a southerly direction towards the point where the Medwyn is joined by the Westruther burn, where we strike a cart-road that

* See p. 58.　　　　　† See p. 57.

L

takes us to the road * between Newbigging and Dunsyre. Less than a mile from Redford bridge we pass,
at some distance to our right, the Wauk Mill,† once
a busy wool mill, now mere ruins, on the banks of the
Medwyn. Passing through Newbigging, we turn to the
right and go by Kaimend to Carnwath.‡

5. *Carnwath and back* viâ *Burn Grange.*

This walk is the same as the last, as far as Parkneuk, at which point we turn to the right and make
for the Wauk Mill, whence, instead of keeping on the
cart-road, we take the foot-path going due east, which,
after crossing the Westruther burn and a little tributary of it, brings us to Burn Grange,§ where a famous
market used to be held. Then we hold southward to
the road between Dunsyre and Newbigging, and
finish the walk as above.

The two walks last described are rights-of-way;
there are, however, hundreds of little tramps that can
be taken throughout the Pentland region which are
not on rights-of-way, but which pedestrians who are
careful to respect the rights of property, and who
avoid the shooting season, may safely take without
fear of molestation. Indeed, unless one is accompanied
by a dog—which friend and companion of man is an

* See p. 84.
† There were many "wauk-mills" in Scotland in the days preceding
the modern developments in machinery. They smoothed and shrank the
rough homespun cloth that came from the cottage looms.
‡ See p. 85.   § See p. 85, *note*.

object of aversion to landlords and shepherds when it belongs to somebody else—one need not fear interruption in crossing any part of the hills.

Whan Spring-time flecks the hillside wi' the bonnie wee lambs,
That skip an' loup like flechs aboot their grey auld dams;
Whan the skirlin' o' the peesweep an' the whaup is heard,
An' the muir-cock cuts his capers to his coy hen-bird;
Whan the laverock birls his teerie-leeries in the blue lift,
An' the sun licks up the bree o' Winter's last snaw-drift;
Whan the scent o' growth comes fragrant frae the fresh pleugh-
    drills,—
Whaur better could ye be than to tak' a walk wi' me
                    Owre the Pentland Hills?

Whan the sky gangs up to heaven in the lang het days,
And the Summer sun is shining wi' his strang het rays;
Whan the swee-zee o' the swallows greets the early morn,
An' the gloamin' hears the crake amang the standin' corn;
Whan the breeze is sweet wi' clover and the new-mown hay,
An' wafts abroad the echoes o' the bairns at play;
Whan the sheer delight o' leevin' a' creation thrills,—
Whaur better could ye be than to tak' a walk wi' me
                    Owre the Pentland Hills?

Whan Autumn's fiery fingers set the woods a-lowe,
An' bind the purple ling aboot the mountain's brow;
Whan the couthie robin redbriest starts his back-end sang,
An' the wild-duck herds her brood on ilka loch an' stang;
Whan Nature sheds the treasures o' her teemin' wame,
Whan the gowden hairst is geddered, an' the clyack brocht
        hame;
Whan merry gang the water-wheels o' monie auld mills,—
Whaur better could ye be than to tak' a walk wi' me
                    Owre the Pentland Hills?

Whan dowie Winter scants her licht wi' laich-hung sun,
An' nicht comes doon afore the day is weel begun;
Whan Nature dons her ice-cuirass wi' mantua o' snaw
An' busks her cockernonie wi' the holly-berries braw;

Whan birds an' beasts creep in aboot to beg their bried,
An' plead wi' ourie, anxious luik their sair time o' need ;
Whan the trees hae tint their leaves, an' a' the flow'rets hide,
Whan auld folk cower an' shiver by the bricht fireside,
Wi' plaids aboot their shouthers, fearin' cauld an' chills,—
Whaur better could ye be than to tak' a walk wi' me
                    Owre the Pentland Hills ?

        If ye seek the best remeid
          For the warst o' warldly ills,
        A tramp is a' ye need
          Owre the Pentland Hills.

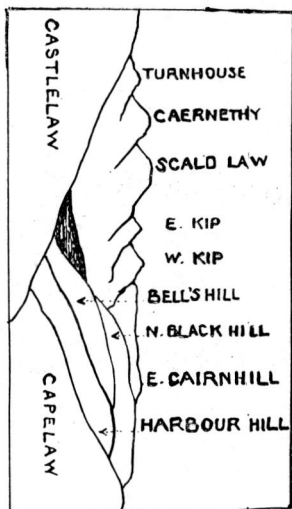

Loganlee Valley from Fala Knowe

[To face page 98

APPENDICES

A

A Glimpse of Pentland in the Thirteenth Century.

There is preserved in the English archives a parchment of no little interest to those who wander about the Pentland range. It dates from the end of the thirteenth century, and gives evidence of the antiquity of not a few local names. The following *résumé* of the parchment is published in the *Calendar of Documents relating to Scotland*, vol. iv. p. 356: " Inquisition made in the Chapel of Saint Katherine on Friday next after the Feast of Saint Peter *ad vincula*, A.D. 1280 (?) [on the] land of Bavelay, by Thomas de Balhernoc, Thomas de Bounayelin, John de Garnhac (?),* Gilbert de ——, Robert de Alton, Richard de Harlau, Alan, son of Elias, Walter de Balhernock, John de —— and John de Galwadra, John de Bradwod, Galfrid de Cotis, Henry 'senescall † de Gorth ' (?), William de Walestun, Thomas 'senescall de Botland,' William, brother of Thomas de Balhernock, Arnald de Listunschelis, Michael 'senescall de Newt' (?) —— [Thomas] de Hardkneys, William de Harlau, Richard Blauhorne, Alexander de Maleny (?), William de

---

* This is possibly the original of Garnock, a family name not uncommon in the Pentland area.

† The "Senescall," at the period of this document, seems to have combined the functions and responsibilities of principal tenant and of land steward.

Balin —— John de Harlau, John Corte, Ranulph Makeles, Thomas Scheipshank (?), William Wode- [man], and Gilbert de Balhernoc, who all sworn and diligently examined, viz., xii of the barony, say that for fifty years 'byegone' and more the K. never had right within the bounds of Baveley which is the lord of Brad's; but the servants of the lords of Brad always took the animals of all the K.'s farmers in the moor of Pentland, and imparked them, and took 'punlayn' whenever they found them within the bounds of Bavelay, and thus all the lords of Brad have ever held that law of Bavelay till the time of Sir William de Sancto Claro, and this because Sir Thomas de Brad demanded 8d. of 'punlayn' from the K.'s men, as the K.'s men have taken 8d. from his men."

Some of the local and family names in the above are easily identified—such as Bavelaw, Bonaly, Harelaw, Braidwood, Coates, Walstone, Listonshiels, Maleny and Baleny (?) which last, I imagine, to be concealed under the name "William de Balin." The lord of Brad is, of course, the laird of Braid. It is interesting to note that the names of so many places that are now large farms figure in this document of the thirteenth century. May the genealogically inexpert ask if Richard Blauhorne be the ancestor of the Pennicuik family, and his name the real origin of the legend, connected with Penicuik House? *

* See *The Royal Hunt of Roslin*, by James Jackson, Edin., 1848. The story makes Bruce say, at the end of the hunt, to Randolph de Clerc—"I make you the grant of the estate of Pennicuik . . . which will march with his (St Clair's) of the Pentland range; and to transmit the recollection of this day to posterity, your estate shall be held in the following terms, viz. : that when I, or any of the succeeding kings of Scotland, shall come to hunt upon the Pentlands or upon Boroughmuir, your forester shall attend at the gathering; and, sitting upon the top of the gathering or Buck's Stane, near Edinburgh, shall wind three blasts of the bugle-horn." (*See* also *Clerk of Pennicuik's Memoirs*, pp. 5, 6). A footnote to the above says—"Sir W. Scott remarks that the

The Clerks bought the Penicuik estate in 1654, John
Clerk,—son of a Montrose merchant,—who made his
fortune in Paris and became a burgess of Edinburgh,
being the purchaser. (See *Clerk of Pennicuik's Memoirs*,
edited by J. M. Gray, 1892). I doubt the authenticity of
the " Free for a Blast " legend, though I brave the wrath
of the Heralds' College in so doing. Still more do I doubt
the legend alluded to in the note on the preceding page.
In matters of heraldry and genealogy, angels rush in
where fools fear to tread, and therefore I am inclined to
trace the arms, the legend, and the honourable traditions
of the successive families that have held the barony of
Penicuik, to good old Richard Blauhorne of the thirteenth
century—before Bruce was king.

B

The Drainage of the Pentlands.

The Pentland range receives and collects during the
year a vast quantity of water, and distributes it over a far
wider area than one might expect from a cursory glance
at its position on the map. Though it lies well to the east
of Scotland, it empties its waters not only into the German
Ocean but also into the Atlantic. The waters of the North
Mass go entirely into the German Ocean *viâ* the Firth of
Forth. Most of these are conveyed by the Water of Leith
and the North Esk River, but a few small streams find

---

barony of Penicuik, the property of Sir George Clerk, Bart., is held by
a singular tenure : the proprietor being bound to sit upon a large rocky
fragment near Edinburgh, called the Buck's Stane, and wind three blasts
of a horn when the king shall come to hunt upon the Boroughmuir ;
hence the family have adopted as their crest a demi-forester proper,
winding a horn, with the motto ' Free for a Blast.' " *Minstrelsy of the
Border*, vol. iii., p. 413.

their way independently to the Forth, between Leith and Musselburgh. The North Central Mass sends its contribution to the sea by the two rivers above named. The drainage of the South Central Mass is partly conveyed to the sea by the same two rivers, partly also by the Lyne, a tributary of the Tweed; while that of the South Mass is carried to the two oceans—on the north side to the German Ocean, *viâ* the Firth of Forth, by the Almond River and the Water of Leith; on the south side to the German Ocean *viâ* the Tweed by the Lyne and its tributaries, and to the Atlantic *viâ* the Clyde by the North and South Medwyn Rivers. Some of the streams flowing in widely different directions have their source within a few yards of each other. Near the Garval Syke (p. 144) three streams rise within a circle less than a mile in diameter, which go to the Forth, the Tweed and the Clyde respectively. Near Garvald House (p. 80) the waters of the South Medwyn are artificially divided, and so narrow is the watershed here that by this diversion part of the water takes its normal route to the Clyde, while the rest makes for the Lyne valley and on to the Tweed.

Reference has already been made (p. 103) to the chain of reservoirs on the hills, most of which supply excellent drinking water to the towns and villages round the Pentland area, and some of which are compensation ponds in the interests of certain mills and factories on the banks of the various streams.

C

Pedestrians' Map (Bartholomew).

I have recommended the use of this map as a companion to the reader. I had made a note of some mistakes in it which were due to Messrs Bartholomew accepting the Ordnance Survey map as correct. It is far from that. I once met an Ordnance surveyor, whose duty was to verify the maps of the district, who asked me where Whim Pond was. He had cycled from Leadburn to Romanno by Noblehouse, and yet—! It was "as invisible as a nose on a man's face, or a weather-cock on a steeple."

In regard to the *Pedestrians' Map*, I may state that in the latest edition all the errors I had noted have been corrected, except that the Black Hill is still named the Black Law, and the real Black Law is called the Bleak Law.

Apart from this trifling error, the map is excellent. I carry it always in my wanderings over the hills, and know it to be most useful. I hope that the publishers will find, in the preceding pages, matter that will enable them to issue future editions with fuller detail. With a scale of 1½ inches to the mile, they have space to place and name a considerable number of interesting spots, endeared, by many pleasant associations, to the Pentland enthusiast.

GLOSSARY

A'—all.
Ae—one.
Ain—own.
Aince—once.
A-lowe—a-flame.
Anaith—under, beneath.
Auld—old.
A-wee—a short time.
Back-end—autumn.
Birkies—young men.
Birks—birch-trees.
Birls—trills, whirrs.
Blate—bashful.
Blithe—gladsome.
Brae—bank, declivity.
Braw—pretty, attractive.
Bree—dregs, juice, gravy.
Breith—breath.
Bried—bread.
Brocht—brought.
Burnie—a small stream.
Busks—decks.
Byre—cowhouse.

Caa—drive.
Callants—young men.
Cauld—cold.
Claes—clothes.
Clyack—the last sheaf at harvest.
Coaties—petticoats.
Cockernonie—head-dress.
Couthie—bold and frank.
Crake—Corn-crake (or land-rail).
Cudna—could not.

Dawtin'—petting, fondling.
Dee—die.
Deece—wooden seat; see p. 72 n.
Doon—down.

Dowie—gloomy, sad.
Drappin'—dropping.
Drumly — muddy, clouded (if liquids).

E'e, Een—eye, eyes.

Fand—found.
Fa's—falls.
Fee—reward.
Ferlies—wonders, marvels.
Flechs—fleas.
Flecks—dots, speckles.
Flowrie—flowery.
Forebriest o' the Laft—Front seat of gallery in Scottish churches.

Gang—go.
Gawsy—buxom.
Geddered—gathered.
Gloamin'—dusk.
Gowden—golden.
Greinin'—longing for, yearning after.

Hairt—heart.
Hairst—harvest.
Hame—home.
Hempie—madcap. (One for whom hemp has been sown with a view to the future).
Het—hot.
Howe—hollow.
Howm—meadow.

Joe—beau, suitor.

Kaim—comb.
Keekin'—peeping.

Kilted—tucked up.
Kye—cows.

Laft—gallery (in church).
Laich-hung—low-hung.
Lane—"her lane," herself alone.
Laverock—lark.
Licht—light.
Lift—sky.
Liltin'—singing.
Lin—waterfall.
Ling—heather.
Linties—linnets (small song-birds in general).
Lissom—slender.
Loan—lane.
Lo'ed—loved.
Loot—let.
Loup—leap.
Loupin'-stane—stone from which a horse is mounted.
Lowe—flame.
Luik—look.

Mair—more.
Mantua—cloak.
Mavis—song-thrush.
Methocht—methought.
Monie—many.
Muir-cock—grouse.

Nicht—night.

Oot-bye—outside.
Ourie—drooping, shivering.
Out-ower—over, outside.
Owre—over.

Peesweep—lapwing.
Pleugh-drills—furrows.

Quean—girl.

Remeid—remedy.
Rins—runs.

Sair—sore.
Shouthers—shoulders.
Skirlin'—screeching.
Smittal—infection or contagion of disease.
Snaw—snow.
Sonsy—plump.
Spuilzie—spoil.
Stang—pond.
Stauns—stands.
Strang—strong.
Swee-zee—onomatopoetic for note of swallow.

Teerie-leeries (Fr. *tiri-liri*)—onomatopoetic for song of lark.
Thocht—thought.
Threipit—urged.
Tint—lost.
Tuik—took.

Verra—very.

Wad—would.
Waefu'—woeful.
Wale—choice, selection.
Wame—womb.
Warst—worst.
Waukens—wakens.
Wean—little one, child.
Whaup—curlew.
Whaur—where.
Wow!—alas!

Yerlane—yellow-hammer.
Yird—earth, soil.

INDEX.

COLSTONS LIMITED, PRINTERS, EDINBURGH